1

"They a mutilate each other as we do. They ask why we hold so little regard for human life. But to ask why we turned from bad to worse is to ignore from whence we came. You see, you wouldn't ask why the rose that grew from the concrete had damaged petals; on the contrary we would all celebrate its tenacity; we would all love its will to reach the sun. Well, I am that rose, this (U.S.A) is the concrete, and these (my experiences) are my damaged petals. Don't ask me why, (it happened) but thank God, and ask me how." (I overcame)"

Tupac Shakur, Ghetto Poet

The Domination of Corruption

The seemingly inherent good or evil that lies within man has been widely discussed and debated over the ages. One theory I prefer over all others is John Locke's *Two Treatises of Government*. In his treatise under the State of Man, Locke states, "If human beings were born without any preexisting qualities their natural state must be one of perfect freedom." Locke goes on to add, "Whether people become brutish or otherwise depended solely on their experiences and their environment."

I will look back over my life and relive each step of my training in an attempt to show how my experiences and environment sent me down a road that eventually led to me getting shot and then to my transformation. This book is not meant to point a finger at or blame anyone. It is just a look into my once innocent mind to see how it became transformed. It would be a lie to say my parents only had a negative influence on my life; in fact, they taught me a lot of positive things that I still live by today. However, as far back as I can remember, my upbringing groomed me to be the opposite of not only my character, but also my true nature.

CHAPTER 1

Learning of Corruption

Ten hours into my mother's labor with my older sister Kim, the doctors realized there were two babies in the womb. Doctors fought to save the life of the second child, but after eighteen hours in the operating room, they emerged with only Kim. My mom sank deep into an abyss of regret, remorse, and then depression. The family was in turmoil, but my dad-- being the loving husband he was-- tried to hold things together. However, the weight of caring for three rambunctious kids and a depressed wife in addition to his responsibilities at work were too overwhelming, and in the end, he succumbed to the pressures.

In a desperate plea for help, my dad drove to the hospital seeking the advice of a doctor. By sheer luck, he ran into the same doctor who delivered Kim in the hallway. The doctor's advice to my dad was: "Get her pregnant, and do it fast." The doctor's reasoning was the only thing that could help my mom get over the loss of her child was the birth of another child. The story told throughout the family is that for the next four months, no one outside the house saw hide or hair of my mom or dad until the announcement came— "I'm pregnant."

I was born on August 11, 1974, in San Francisco, California, and was given the name Frederick Robert Howard Jr. by my mother, Marsha Howard. Unlike in the

stories today of single mothers and deadbeat dads, I lived
with both my parents every day of my life until I ran
away. I was the fourth child of the Howard family, and
due to the circumstances surrounding my conception, I
became my mom's favorite. The oldest of the kids was
Shawn. at 5'6" and 138 lbs., she was the shield and
sword that protected us from the dangers and kids
outside the house. Due to this, my dad gave her the
nickname "Bruiser". Shawn was a beautiful caramel-
complexioned young lady, and because she had long hair
and a pretty face, the boys of the neighborhood were
always at our house. Shawn's beauty was second only to
her bad attitude, which always kept her ready to fight.

Next in line was Richard. Standing a towering
6'1" and at about 150 lbs., he was my guardian when I
left the house. Where he went so did I, my mom often
commanded. Richie was really smart, but he feared
everyone except me. I often wondered why he didn't like
to fight but never questioned him about his fear. Richie's
defining feature was his head, which was a source of
torment for him in school. His head sloped in the front
and was straight up in the back, which gave the
appearance of a cone. His dark-skinned, muscular frame
was never interesting to the girls, but he didn't mind too
much. He was only interested in making money.

Then there was Kim, the third child; she was
quiet and shy and hardly ever spoke or went outside

because she was afraid of the other kids. Like Richie, Kim was teased throughout school because she had an overwhelming overbite. On her skinny frame, the overbite was the first thing people would notice. Kim stood about 5'4" but weighed only 100 lbs. She was dark-skinned and had hair like wool. Although at her core she was filled with love and compassion for others, no one knew because she was so shy and withdrawn. Kim was always our lookout when we were up to mischief.

Then there was me, the baby boy, the miracle child. I would remain the baby of the family until Chantia arrived three years later. My mom gave me the nickname "Tootie" at birth. It just so happened that it was also the name of a girl on the hit TV show *The Facts of Life*. Therefore, growing up I always felt as if I had something to prove. No matter how dangerous or absurd the dare, I always took it, and it always ended in a butt-whipping. Like Shawn, I had a caramel complexion, but unlike the rest of the family I was born with two deep dimples on each side of my face. I stood 5' and weighed 93 lbs. at 7 years old, but my heart and courage made me feel as if I was 10' tall. At an early age, I learned quickly to watch, listen, and learn in all my surroundings and situations. Due to the fact that training started early in the Howard family, we needed to be attentive and absorb the lessons from our surroundings, parents, and each other quickly in order to avoid a butt-whipping,.

My mom at 5'2" and 119 lbs., was the dominant
presence in the house, and my dad was her backup. My
mom looked a lot like Cicely Tyson, with a brown sugar
complexion, slim figure, and perfectly proportioned face,
which made her beautiful. When it came to my mom, the
older kids had to watch every word and facial
expression, because she was always looking for the
slightest sign of disrespect. Shawn was the only child
who challenged my mom openly. As I think back on the
characters of my siblings and myself as children and the
way in which my parents chose to train us, I see a direct
correlation with Shawn's anger, Richie's lack of
courage, and Kim's fearfulness.

Shawn's anger came from the responsibilities that
my mom laid on her at an early age. Shawn had to cook,
get us up and dressed for school, and make sure we
cleaned the house, including our rooms. She was more
of a parent to us than my mom and dad in my eyes.
However, Shawn was a fifteen-year-old girl who was
interested in boys and her friends, and these
responsibilities limited the time she could devote to her
own interests, which brought about resentments. These
resentments built up and spilled out in mumblings and
back talking, but my mom always brought about order
with pain.

I remember one evening Shawn was in the
window talking to a boy. When my mom overheard her,

she asked Shawn, "Did you help Kim and Tootie with their homework?"

Shawn turned to face my mom and said, "They not my kids!"

With the speed of a greyhound and the ferocity of a charging rhino, my mom attacked her, and when the dust had cleared, Shawn lay on the floor with a busted lip and a bruised left eye. Shawn picked herself up and hobbled into our room to do what my mom should have been doing.

Instances like this were common in the Howard household, but we were bound to a code that kept us in the same situation. From the time we were able to speak my mom pounded into us that what happened in the house stayed in the house. For our parents, this code was a shield that protected them, but for us, it meant we had to suffer in silence. Richie tried once to reveal what was going on in the home, but my mom talked her way out of it, and the butt-whipping he got for it put the fear of God in all of us.

Richie's lack of courage was instilled in him through butt-whippings and intimidation carried out by my mom and dad. Any time Richie got up the nerve to challenge a rule or a command, he was swiftly and mercilessly dealt with. My mom's authority was maintained through fear, and Richie's 6'1" frame was a silent threat to the status quo. My mom believed that if a child disrespected her or was disobedient to her, the way to get them to mind was to apply pain, and if they continued a wrong course, apply more pain. My mom's punishments were so severe that Richie came to fear the very thought of pain in all its forms. I recall one situation while we were living in Oakland. There were always kids who challenged each other to fights to prove who was the toughest. No one messed with me because I was always up for a fight, but Richie was a different story.

One day my mom yelled into our room, "Richie and Shawn, get down here!"

As Shawn and Richie ran down the stairs, they both yelled back, "Yes!"

My mom pointed to money lying on the coffee table. "I need y'all to go to the store to get a loaf of bread, and please don't bring me back no white bread."

As they walked back home, they encountered three boys about Richie's age who wanted Richie to fight. One boy said, "What's up, Rich-nard?"

Richie immediately said, "I didn't say it."

Shawn, unaware of what was happening, asked, "Say what?"

Before Richie could answer, one of the boys swung and missed, but his intent was enough for Shawn to drop the bread and attack the boy. The other two boys jumped in, but Richie had seen all he needed to, and he turned and ran while Shawn fought all three boys.

When I later asked Richie why he ran, he said, "I didn't want to be hit."

A phobia he overcame in his later years. However, this began a cat and mouse game between Richie and the boys of the neighborhood where we lived. Anytime they would see Richie they would chase him. Richie's only sanctuary was in the confines of the front yard. We all had our quirks and limitations placed on us by the environment and our upbringing, but Kim had it the worst by my standards.

Shawn, Richie, and I never had any trouble making friends, but Kim's shyness was a great hindrance to her social development. The fear of upsetting my mom was a great motivator to keep silent around the house. My mom prescribed to the notion that children should be seen and not heard, and Kim bought into it wholeheartedly. Kim's willingness to be silent around the house made it easy to carry the same behavior outside the house as well. One summer day while most of the parents of the neighborhood were at work, my siblings got into an argument with another family's kids. The Johnson family had a girl we called "Big Kim" and her sister Teresa; my family had Shawn and Kim.

The four girls matched off as Big Kim yelled, "Shawn, I'm gon' beat yo' ass!"

Shawn shouted back, "You might know karate, but it ain't gon' help you. Your ass is mine, bitch!"

The fight between Shawn and Big Kim lasted only a couple of minutes. They went around in a circle for a few minutes, then with a facial expression that could have killed a cat, Big Kim did a sweeping roundhouse kick, and Shawn, the street brawler that she was, grabbed Big Kim's leg, picked her up, and slammed her to the ground.

Big Kim yelled, "Get off me and let's start fresh!"

Shawn said, "No, you wanted to fight, bitch, so let's fight!"

Big Kim called out to her sister, "Teresa, get this bitch off of me!"

As Teresa started to grab Shawn's foot to drag her off her sister, Shawn said to our Kim, "Kim, you better beat her ass!"

The problem was Kim was nowhere to be found, so after the fight we searched all over the neighborhood for Kim but could not find her. Once it started to get dark and there was still no Kim, we began to worry. Shawn called my mom and told her we could not find Kim.

My mom asked, "What happened? Did y'all check all through the house?"

Shawn said, "Yeah, she not here."

My mom said, "Check again, and call me back."

After we searched again, Shawn called my mom back. "We still can't find her."

My mom, knowing her daughter, asked, "Did y'all check under the beds?"

Shawn said, "No, why?"

My mom said, "Check and call me back."

We found Kim under her bed sound asleep. Shawn yelled at Kim, "Why you under the bed?"

We all knew it was because she was afraid to fight, and she knew if Shawn had found her she would have made her fight. Kim's lack of heart caused her many problems as a child, but my oversized heart may have caused me just as many, if not more, problems.

I remember at age six wondering about the strange light emanating from the box my mother used to prepare our food, which I later learned was the stove. I was big enough to reach the top of it, and on more than one occasion I tried to touch the fire but was always prevented by someone older.

One day when my mom wasn't home and Shawn was cooking, I just happened to walk by the kitchen.

Shawn asked, "Tootie, you hungry?"

I said, "Yeah."

As she turned to make my plate, the dazzling fire drew me in like a moth to the light. Slowly I reached up and tried again to touch the fire.

Shawn yelled out, "Stop! Daddy, Tootie's trying to touch the fire again."

My dad, a stocky, brown-skinned man of about thirty-five, said with his sternest face, "Let him touch it."

Trembling because of my dad's face and because everyone came to watch, but at the same time filled with excitement, adrenaline, and relief, I slowly reached for the fire. At first, as my hand entered the flame, I just felt warmth that intrigued me, but as my hand stayed in the fire, an intense burning replaced fascination, and all at once I both screamed and cried.

Richie yelled, "Dummy!"

Then Kim said, "That's what you get!"

Everyone laughed, and for the next three weeks Richie and Kim took turns asking me if I wanted to touch the fire again. As I look back, this is where two of my most corrupt morals were formed. In that moment I learned *it is funny when other people get hurt, and trials, difficulties, and pain are the victim's fault.* These two morals were the first two stones laid in the foundation of my corruption. Before this time, I felt sad if others were crying, and I often went to defend them. However, there would be other morals and values to come that would turn an otherwise thoughtful, generous, honest, truthful kid into a selfish, stingy, deceitful liar.

After the experience with the fire, I became distrustful of my family and, to some extent, even of myself. Even though I didn't understand the meaning of love, I often wondered why my friends and their siblings did things that mine didn't. Most of my friends who had big brothers were protected and helped by them. Richie and I were close, but every chance he got he would beat on me. If he wasn't throwing me across the room, he would smother me with pillows or blankets, which for a seven-year-old was terrifying.

One day as I entered the room Richie and I shared, he was lying on his bed. When he looked up and saw me, I instantly knew, but it was too late.

Richie said, "Tootie, you want to wrestle?"

At that time, I was about a foot shorter than he was, so I tried to back up, but like a hungry lion he pounced. Before I knew it, I was the helpless victim of a DDT— a violent chokehold where you slam your opponent's head into the floor. If that wasn't bad enough, when I got up the nerve to go and tell my parents, I was told to stop being a tattletale. Through this experience, the third and fourth morals were added to my character: *prey on those weaker than you,* and *never tell on anyone.* These principles were contrary to my earlier character. Up until that time, I was a defender of those weaker than me and felt telling was the only way to get help. At the time, I made no conscious decision to change, but unconsciously I adapted to my environment.

THE TWO PATHS

In 1982, at the tender age of eight, I was unleashed upon the streets of Oakland, California, and my mind soaked up all that was around me. My desire to prove myself found a playground not full of friends but tests. Until then I had never had a fight, unless you count the merciless beatings I took from Richie.

My first day outside, a kid named Tommy came up to me and asked, "What's your name?"

"My name is Tootie," I answered.

After his next words, which were, "That's a girl's name," I had my first fight.

Due to my courage and heart, the older kids took a liking to me and let me in their circle. So, while other kids my age were playing tag and hide-and-go-seek, I was sitting on the porch of the young drug dealers in the neighborhood. Vonne and Isaac were the two young men who protected me and supplied me with change to go to the store. These brothers were twins who stood 6'5" and topped the scales at a cool 280 lbs. They terrorized the neighborhood. Both were light-skinned African American young men with golden blond hair and attitudes that said they didn't care for no one but each other. One day, a man came to the porch mad about something.

Vonne calmly said, "Lower your voice."

Not understanding what was about to happen, I sat and watched.

The man said, "Fuck that!"

Like a predator showing no remorse as it viciously attacks its prey, Vonne leapt off the porch, and before I could process what was happening, the man was on the ground yelling, "Help!"

That day my fifth and six morals were formed: *Never let anyone try to get over on me*, and *always* react *with violence.*

So, when Richie beat me up, I would just wait until we went outside, then I would tell Vonne, and he would beat Richie up for me. After two or three beatings from Vonne, Richie stopped messing with me and started to be my friend. As children from a poor family, we banded together because when people are born into poverty, they learn quickly that making allies is the easiest way to find a hustle. Our hustle came from what most would think was an unlikely source, but my dad led us down the path step by step.

While I was in elementary school, my dad worked at the Mother's Cookies factory in Oakland, California. During those times, our house was always full of all kinds of cookies. Being a kid, I never questioned why, until one night my mom woke Richie and me up at about 11:00 PM and said, "Get dressed, I need y'all help."

When it came to my mom and her commands, we learned early not to ever question her—only to obey. Once dressed, we ran to the living room for further instructions. My mom then said, "Go get in the car." Like good little soldiers we obeyed. After a fifteen-minute drive around the snack industry warehouses in our neighborhood and a short walk, we arrived at the back door of the Mother's Cookies factory.

My dad emerged from a side door and motioned for us to come closer. Unaware of what was happening, I followed my mom. Once we were at the door, all was revealed because I saw boxes of cookies. My dad started to hand them to Richie and me and said, "Run these to the car and come back for the rest."

It wasn't until we got home and safe in our room that Richie told me, "Daddy is stealing those cookies, Tootie."

I could not believe it. The man who had whipped us countless times for stealing was himself stealing. If I had known the word, I would have said, "Hypocrite!" This is where my seventh moral took root: *If you wanted something and had the opportunity, then it was okay to take it (or steal it).*

As my graduation from elementary school approached, my dad came home one evening, and he and my mom headed for their room. Richie and I ran to the back door because there we had a bird's-eye view of my parents' room.

First my mom said, "Fred, what s up?"

Then we heard my dad say, "I got fired."

I asked Richie, "What does 'fired' mean?"

He said, "It means you not getting that new suit or those new shoes for graduation."

It took the kids four months to really find out what happened, but in such a close living space there's no such thing as a secret.

One day while my mom was on the phone, Kim came running into the room and said, "Mommy's talking about it on the phone" — "it" being my dad's firing.

We all jumped up, ran into the kitchen, and sat at the table with the cards. We brought the cards along because if my mom thought we were eavesdropping, we would get a butt-whipping for the ages.

When we arrived, we heard my mom say, "He was stupid for taking all those cookies." Then it got silent, so we started dealing the cards for our cover story. Mom said, "We ain't paid rent in two months."

Shawn got worried and told us, "We about to be evicted again."

"Again?" I asked.

She just shook her head and walked to her room.

Eviction day came like a mighty earthquake that shook not only the family as a whole, but each individual member to the core. I had not been aware during the last three evictions, but I was fully awake for this one. It was just like what I had seen on TV. The police came out to make sure we would leave peacefully. We had to pack up the car with all that we could carry—mostly food, blankets, and some of our clothes—while we watched the rest being slung into the streets. Our life's material accumulations were gone. I learned my most important value in this experience: *Without money you* are *left to the mercy of others,* so *value money above everything else.*

The next two years were uncertain times. No one knew where the family would sleep or even if there would be food to eat. Many nights we went to bed with no food, and there were times that we didn't sleep. My mom kept our spirits high for the most part, but Shawn and Richie could not be comforted. They missed their friends, schools, and belongings. We stayed in hotels. Some were by the week and some were by the month, but we always had to leave on the twenty-eighth day. This was done so the managers would not have to go through the eviction process, but they maintained the right to make us leave anytime they wanted us to. They did this often because our family was so big that no manager wanted us in one room, but we could not afford two rooms. My dad's solution was to send my mom and Kim in to rent the room and then send the rest of us to the room one by one until we all had made it in. His solution only worked half of the time. The rest of the time we would have to get out on the spot.

I remember one night we were awakened to a banging on the door. Everyone sat up as my dad went to the door then turned and said, "It's the manager."

My mom jumped up and rushed us into the bathroom.

Through the door of the bathroom, we heard a man say, "I know you have too many people in there. I warned you, now get out!"

My dad and mom yelled back, "Give us our money back and we will leave!" They never gave our money back, but we always had to leave.

That night we were left with nothing but distress. My mom turned and asked my dad, "What now?"

His reply was, "I don't know."

As children, we looked to our parents, but at that moment I wondered who do they look to? My mom turned to us and asked, "Who wants to go camping?"

Kim and I yelled out together, "I do! I do!"

Richie and Shawn asked, "What? We gon' sleep in the park?"

It just so happened that across the street from the hotel was a park that had a big play structure. Kim and I cuddled together under one big blanket and looked up at the stars until we fell asleep, and by the attitude of the family, no one would have guessed that we were homeless. That was the first night we spent outside. That situation formed my next value: *He who has the power controls the people,* and *when you gain power show no compassion. And so I coveted power.*

The next morning brought with it the problems of where to find shelter and how to feed the kids. All the food we had had spoiled because it sat out all night. At about 6:00 AM, I heard my dad say to my mother, "You take the girls to the Salvation Army to get the voucher and I'll take Richie and Tootie to get the food."

When the sun came up, the family packed up and each squad went their way to carry out their assigned tasks. When my dad told Richie and me that we were going to get food, we would have never guessed his method.

While walking to Safeway, my dad told Richie, "You get the rice and sugar," and then looked at me and said, "Tootie, you get the Kool-Aid."

Richie needed no further instructions. He knew what to do, but I looked up to my dad and with the innocence of a child, and I said, "Daddy, I need some money."

He looked back at me with pity mixed with sadness and regret and said, "Tootie, just put it in your pocket and then hurry up and leave the store."

As we entered the store, we split up. As I stood in front of the Kool-Aid stand, I remember that I felt neither happy nor sad I was stealing. It was just the thought of what would happen if I didn't do it that ran through my mind. My eighth and ninth moral came by way of our poverty: *Provide for your family no matter what the cost, and never to be afraid to break the law to do it.* Looking back, I don't know how or why they didn't just give up, but I'm glad they didn't because through their toil they raised us.

With homelessness came a bonus for us kids. We didn't have to go to school since we never knew where we would be staying from night to night, and we didn't have all of our clothes or the ability to clean the ones we were wearing. Yet, our time during the day wasn't idle. The girls followed my mom to different shelters and agencies looking for a place to spend the night or for vouchers for hotels. Richie and I spent our time with my dad taking anything that wasn't nailed down. We took car batteries, scrap metal, potatoes from the Granny Goose factory, and anything else we could sell or eat. We never questioned if what we were doing was wrong because we could all see our need. It wasn't talked about to us, but we heard our parents talking and just knew it was either this, or we would starve.

I remember one summer day in 1986—I was about twelve years old—and my dad, Richie, and I were out on the hunt but came up dry. So, my dad came up with the idea of going by the Granny Goose Factory before we went home. We had never been there before, and Richie and I didn't understand why we were headed that way but kept silent. As we were walking, my dad started instructing us about what we were to do once we arrived at the factory. He looked at Richie and said, "Richie, you lift up the gate for Tootie." Then he turned to me and said, "Tootie, you slide under the gate and go pick up the potatoes off the ground and bring them to us."

It seemed simple enough, but what he forgot to explain was that there would be men walking around that I would have to avoid.

Once we got to the gate, all went well, just like my dad thought. There were a plethora of potatoes all around. Richie, ever so mindful of remembering and following instructions, did exactly as my dad had commanded and lifted up the gate. I was terrified, unsure, and trembling, but I slowly slid under the gate. Now, standing on the opposite side of right, I looked back through the gate at Richie and my dad safe from danger on the other side of the gate, and hated I that I was small. I guess my dad could see the hesitancy in my steps, so he barked through the gate, "Go get them!"

That was the push I needed—the thought of disappointing him shook me, and I ran to pick up the potatoes. Here is where my eleventh moral was formed: *Stealing is only wrong if you get caught because that meant you did it wrong.*

Chapter 2

Internalizing Corruption

Some may fault my parents for my corruption, but each man or woman must choose their own paths. Before homelessness struck, my mom tried her best to create in me a balance of good and bad but left it to me to choose. By the time 1987 rolled around, and I reached the ripe age of thirteen, I was full of corrupt morals and values, but they were not the sum of my foundation. There were also good principles at my core, which battled with the bad morals within me. At thirteen, I spent most of my time out of the reach of my parents' watchful eyes. In the neighborhood, I felt free to explore each path before me. Since I was poor, I didn't have the new shoes or clothes that other kids wore, but I desperately wanted them. Therefore, poverty's temptations sped around me like the mighty flow of a great river, and with only my childish understanding to do combat, I succumbed to its waves.

In the neighborhood, there were many kids doing what was considered right, but there were just as many doing what could be considered wrong. It was my decision to follow those with questionable characters. I remember the summer before I was to enter the seventh grade. I can honestly say I made my choice during this period. That summer, I had made friends with the cool kids; they were brothers named Otis and Cesare. These two boys dressed like they were rich but spent food stamps like all of us poor kids.

So, one day while we were out riding our bikes, I asked Otis, "How much did you pay for them shoes?"

Otis—a tall, lanky, blond-haired, light-skinned black kid who was the older of the two but always followed Cesare—said, "Eighty dollars."

Out of nowhere, Cesare yelled out, "He lying! He stole them shoes!"

I remember I felt surprised, but at the same time it intrigued me, and I turned to Cesare and asked, "How?"

Cesare said, "It's easy; all we do is wear some tore up shoes to J.C. Penney and then put on the new shoes and leave the old ones in the box."

Otis chimed in and said, "They don't even have alarms, and the side door is there for us to walk right out."

After their explanation, I asked, "Can y'all take me?"

Cesare said, "Yeah, but you got to be ready early because that's the best time."

That night I could not sleep; the thoughts of Nike shoes danced in my head like belly dancers on the tables of an emperor. Would I get red Nikes? No, maybe blue. Then I thought even better: I would choose blue and red. The next morning, I was up at 6:00 AM, dressed by 6:15 AM, and out the door by 6:30 AM. To my disappointment, Otis and Cesare were still asleep when I got to their house. So, I passed the time going to the basketball court where all the kids hung out shooting hoops. As I walked, I decided to find the shoes I would steal by first judging the shoes of the kids at the court. When I arrived, there were three kids playing, but I didn't like any of their shoes. I remember feeling eager and frustrated at the same time. After about two hours, I found them. To my surprise, I didn't pick Nikes—Filas caught my eyes instead. They were all white with red, blue, and black lines running down the sides. I ran to Otis and Cesare's house with the anticipation of a runner at the starting line of a race, waiting to hear the gunfire. And fire it did. As I approached their house, their door opened and out they came.

Even though I had only stolen things to feed the family, the thought that it was okay to take what you didn't have was already imbedded in my young character. I was scared, but I didn't want to stop. All the way there I could only think of the benefit, never considering what would happen if I got caught. Once at the store, Otis said, "We got to go in one at a time so they don't see us."

Cesare went in first, then it was my turn. As soon as I turned down the second row, I spotted them. I went straight for the boxes and grabbed a size 4, put them on, and, remembering my dad's instructions at Safeway, I immediately left the store. I thought I got in and out fast, but when I got to the meetup spot Otis and Cesare were already there. At the time, I thought getting away was something good. Looking at it now with a hint of wisdom, I realize it was the worst thing that could have happened—because while stealing food satisfies hunger, stealing clothes and shoes satisfies the ego, and like the belly, it will always need to be fed. *This was the first time my corrupt morals had benefited only me, but it wouldn't be the last.* So, I stole all of my school clothes and shoes throughout junior high school.

Stealing became my way of life. I had gotten so good at stealing and lying to cover it up that Kim followed me one day. When I asked her why, she said, "I want to become friends with the kids whose parents are buying you all this stuff."

That was my cover story.

I burst out laughing, turned to face the store, pointed, and said, "There they are!"

She looked really hard then said, "Which ones are their parents?"

I pointed to the sign of the store and said, "Look up there— these are the parents who gave me all that stuff," but Kim still looked puzzled. I looked her right in the eyes and said, "Don't tell Mommy or Daddy, but I'm stealing those clothes, Kim."

Her first words to me revealed the beginning of our upbringing, because she said, "Ooooh, Tootie, if Mommy finds out you gonna get it." Then her second words revealed our reality because she said, "How you do it?"

After a quick explanation, she was willing and ready to try.

Before we walked in the store I said, "Kim, find what you want quickly, put it in your coat, and hurry up out the store."

She said "Okay" but left my sight and did the exact opposite.

I went in and knew where to go and what I was in there for. I quickly picked up some blue jeans and a black tee shirt and left. I waited for Kim at the meetup spot but after twenty minutes and no Kim, I feared she had been caught. So, I left my clothes under a bush and went to go find her. When I entered the store, all looked calm, so I went to the girl's section. I couldn't believe what I saw next: Kim had six or seven outfits in her hands, and she was still looking for more.

I looked around to see if anyone was watching us, then asked her, "Kim, what the hell are you doing!"

She looked at me and said, "I can't decide on the pink or the red."

I thought this was unbelievable. "Kim, this stuff ain't free!"

I then yanked the clothes out of her hands and dragged her out the store with nothing. All the way home Kim threatened me about telling our parents if I didn't take her back tomorrow. Kim and I became closer because of the secret we shared and the benefit that came by way of that secret, but what we didn't know at the time was that we would have to say good-bye to the circuit of stores we frequented, our circle of friends, and even the city we lived in in the coming months.

Once again, the family was threatened with homelessness because sometime during my seventh grade, my parents started to smoke crack. Up until that time, we were only down on our luck, but once drugs entered the scene, we became without hope. Who could really say why they chose to partake of the devil's medicine, but one thing I know for sure: it didn't help our situation. So, one day my mom came into the living room where we kids were watching TV and stated, "We are moving back to San Francisco."

We were so unprepared to hear that kind of news that Richie blurted out, "Fuck!"

All my mom said was, "Deal with it."

By this time Shawn had left home, Richie was looking for his way out, Kim was a young woman dealing with boys, and I had become just the fourth child due to fact that in 1977 my mom had given birth to my younger sister, Chantia, who now was the baby. Chantia was three years younger than me--a sweet, round-faced, chubby little kid. We could not get her to steal, lie, fight, or stop following us around for anything. Chantia became Kim's responsibility: where Kim went, so did Chantia. Even though Chantia wasn't a boy like I desperately wanted her to be, I happily took on the role of big brother, and where we went next, she would need one.

Up until the move, we lived and were homeless in the suburbs of San Francisco in cities like San Mateo and Redwood City, but our parents up and moved us into the heart of San Francisco, the inner city, to what is called the Tenderloin. The Tenderloin was a city inside the city. It is thirty square blocks and sits in the center of downtown San Francisco. It is lined with slumlord motels and filled with drug addicts. The streets were covered with filth, urine, and old gum, which made the concrete look black instead of grey. It was called the financial district for drug dealers because, like Wall Street, it is where hood commodities were bought and sold. The streets were always full of young men and women who were dealing drugs and smoking cigarettes and weed. The homeless lined the walls of the buildings, as well as drug addicts who bought dope in the open. There were certain blocks we could not walk down because addicts smoked crack and shot heroin right outside.

The Tenderloin was divided up into sections. Some blocks were where weed was sold, and other blocks were where crack was sold. At the top of the Tenderloin was where the prostitutes were, and at the bottom was where they sold pills. There was also a corner where the older men and women sold and shot heroin. The Tenderloin was also divided by race. The Asians had their corners, the Latinos had theirs, and the Blacks had their corners, so, it was full of different cultures, foods, religions, and languages. Each group had their own overflow of kids running the streets of the neighborhood.

Before we moved, I had only known pampered preppie kids of whom I had always been the toughest, but the kids of this neighborhood were hard and had been fighting and playing hoops since they were able to walk. I looked, acted, and felt out of place. I was like a fish out of water that everyone laughed at. My speech, manners, and even my stolen clothes were all different from those around me, and they let me know it. The one cool thing was that there was a big park right in the middle of the neighborhood, and it had a basketball court. There was also a loving and compassionate female coach named Ja'net, who always rounded up the kids for basketball leagues.

The leagues were fun and it gave the kids a chance to get to know each and every boy in the neighborhood, which helped me make friends. While playing in a tournaments game, I stole the ball, but it got loose, so I chased it down and even dove to keep it inbounds. After the game, one of the teenagers who helped out, Henry, patted me on the back and said, "Way to hustle out there."

All the kids looked up to Hen because he was a real lady's man, fought really well, and could really play some ball. Hen was about 5'7", a handsome young man with a muscular body type. He was known for having one of the best curly high top fades in the neighborhood. Hen was a lady's man not just because of his pretty face and muscular tone, but also because of his ability to manipulate the minds of the girls who loved him.

He had a brother named Jay-Jay who was my age, and over the months, Jay-Jay and I became good friends. Jay-Jay was a slim young man of average height.

He wasn't as handsome as Hen, but he did all right with the ladies. Jay-Jay wore his hair in corn rolls that hung past his shoulders. The ladies of the neighborhood always wanted to braid his hair, which gave him his way into their pants.

I credit the friendship between Jay-Jay and me with the blossoming of the seeds of my corruption. In the suburbs, I was the only kid stealing, so it was nothing to be proud of or brag about, but *in the inner-city, stealing was a badge of honor*. This badge I wore with pride. The inner city was a breeding ground for corruption. The principles I adopted as a kid—*preying on the weak, never telling on anyone, not trust*ing *others, and stealing only* being *bad if you got caught—were the norm in this environment.* It wasn't because the inner-city kids were any different from the kids in the suburbs, but because the need and desperation led to many of them succumbing to the temptations of the streets. Very few resisted or overcame these temptations without the help of a compassionate and loving mentor who was able and willing to provide for them. However, there were more needy kids than there was available help, so most kids took the route of stealing, selling dope, or selling weed, which furthered the corruption we dealt with.

Initiation into the streets

At the end of my ninth-grade year, I met a group of Asian boys in San Francisco who let me hang out with them. There was "Bo-Lo" the leader, who was short and stocky, with fair skin and a temper that always silenced even the mightiest of foes. The next in line was "Trade", a 4'8" Cambodian with long hair and a mouth that always had us fighting. "Loa" was the artist who tagged our names everywhere; he was tall and slender but was always up for a fight. We spent the hours we were supposed to be in school stealing cars to sell for money. Each of us could get into and hotwire a car in less than five minutes. I know this because we often timed each other.

At different times we would meet up with other kids who also stole cars. For the most part, we kept to ourselves and protected each other from the gangs that roamed the high school. When the order was too big for us to handle, we would allow others to come with us. One day Bo-Lo entered the circle and said, "We got to get twelve cars today."

Everyone said all at once, "How in the hell we gon' do that!"

The most cars we had stolen in one day was eight, and that took all day. Stealing cars was easy, but most of our time went into finding them because we had special cars we were looking for. Bo-Lo's solution was to allow this white boy who had been trying to get in on the action to come with us. His name was John; he was tall, lanky, and never stopped bragging about how fast he was when it came to stealing cars, but to us he was unproven.

After we met up with John, Bo-Lo said to him, "You get the first car," and everybody agreed. While we were looking for the car, John kept talking. He turned to me, the slowest of the bunch, and said, "Watch and learn, my nigga."

I instinctually blurted out, "If you don't do it in less than five minutes, we fighting!"

Bo-Lo said nothing. He just gave me a look that said it would be fine with him. After about an hour, we spotted the Acura we were looking for.

John went to work; he got past the first stage quickly by opening the doors, but he faltered with the alarm and we sat in a car that wasn't ours with the alarm going off for two to three minutes. At this point, Bo-Lo was questioning John and his decision to let him come.

Looking at John, Bo-Lo said, "What's up, man? I thought you knew what you were doing."

John, now sweating and looking puzzled, barked back, "Give me a minute. I almost got it!"

Just then, an old lady with a small child walked up to the car and shouted, "What are y'all doing in there? That's my car!"

We all jumped out and ran back to the school, hoping to lose her in the crowds of teenagers who were out for lunch. Experience had taught me that if I were to get caught, my best bet was not to tell, but once again I got away and lived to feed my corruption again the next day.

As I grew, the principles that were formed in my youth became second nature as a young adult. No longer was I making logical decisions, but now I was just reacting impulsively—which almost always never turned out positively for others. There was a situation that arose in my fourth year of high school that gave me the okay to drop out of school.

During the after-school hours, all the high school seniors would go the Peniel Recreation Center to shoot hoops and play video games. One day, some of the Asian young men felt we were cheating at basketball—which was the truth—but they could not prove it, so we were allowed to stay on the court. These young men secretly plotted to retaliate, and it wasn't on the court that they chose to avenge themselves. That night after Peniel had closed, we went and hung on our usual corner.

Out the corner of his eye, Jay-Jay spotted something and said, "Ey y'all, there's someone in the street."

So, we all got in the street to see, but Hen yelled out, "Run!"

The Asians from Peniel were strapped with bats, sticks, pipes, and sharpened screwdrivers to come pay us back. Everyone broke out and ran, and that day I felt defeated, but mostly I felt like a sucker for running.

Once we got away, I remembered that one of the Asian young men was in my first period P.E. class, and I planned to have my own payback. I arrived at P.E. early and waited for him to show up. About twenty minutes into class, he did. I wanted to really hurt him, so I brought my dad's "Nigga-Knocker" (a short thick stick with tape around the bottom). Once class was over, I waited outside the gym, and when he came out I ran up on him and punched him in the face. He then pulled out a sharpened screwdriver and started at me, so I pulled out the stick, but it dropped. When I looked up, all I saw was that my furious classmate this mad, crazed Asian now had both weapons and was charging. When he got close enough to do some damage, a basketball player saved me. The basketball player was so tall that he picked him up off the ground and held him in the air until the vice principal came. This antic boosted my rep, but it greatly hurt me, because now all the Asians of the neighborhood were trying to kill me.

Because the threat to my life was real, I spent more time around the house. On one hand, staying home saved my life, but on the other hand it pushed my corruption to a height I would have never imagined it could get to. Before that time, Chantia, and I had not spent much time together. She had her friends and her life, and I had mine, but we always knew we could talk to each other if the need arose. Chantia would usually be asleep when I came home before "the threat", and I never asked if she had eaten or not. However, when I started spending more time home, I realized that many nights she had gone to bed hungry. Now that it was only me and Chantia left living at home, I told her if there was any time she couldn't find *food* in the house, she was to tell me, and I would handle it. One night after leaving a friend's house, I arrived home and found Chantia crying.

I asked her, "What's the matter, Chantia?"

She said, "Mommy and Daddy spent all the money, and now we can't go shopping for school clothes."

I didn't really care about school clothes because I had dropped out of school after the fight, but I did feel for her. She turned to me and said, "Here."

With an outstretched hand, she tried to hand me a crisp twenty-dollar bill. Grabbing the money, I asked, "What's this?"

She said, "Mommy told me to give you it, and she gave me one too."

As I sat there holding the money, a thought ran through my mind: *always provide for your family, and never be afraid to break the law to do it.* I looked over at Chantia, who was still sobbing. I remembered how it felt to go to school with the same clothes from last year, and I decided to do something about it.

I moved closer to Chantia and asked her, "Tia, do you trust me?"

With tears still in her eyes she looked deep into my eyes, as if she were searching my very soul, and said, "Yes, Tootie, I do."

I smiled and said, "Give me your twenty. I promise you will have some new school clothes come Monday." She handed me her money and I told her, "Don't tell anyone what we talked about."

"Do I ever?" She said as I sneaked out the window.

Once I touched down on the curb, I thought to myself, *"please, let AJ be outside,"* and then I ran off into the night.

I found my friend AJ standing outside of Boedecker Park in the Tenderloin and immediately asked, "AJ, can I get some plug?" (Plug was double my money in dope.)

AJ was a 5'9" dark-skinned man who never wanted me to be in the streets. He was one of the men who I counted on when I needed to buy food for Tia.

His first words after my question were, "Man, don't do it; just stay in school and play that ball."

I said, "AJ, I just need it to help my sister and then I'm gonna stop."

AJ just shook his head, reached into his bag, and gave me triple my money in dope. I didn't understand at the time why he shook his head because I really thought it would only be once. What I couldn't see was that AJ was living a dreadful life with felony convictions, no education, and no marketable skills; he was trapped in a reality he hated, and he didn't want to damn me to that same existence. I realize now that AJ knew the call of the streets, once heard, would always captivate the listener.

Some say in everything there's a choice for either good or bad, but for me it was either bad or worse. I could have chosen to let my sister suffer at the hands of cruel kids, but for me that was unthinkable. So, I chose the lesser of the two evils in selling drugs. At the time, I thought with the mind of a child, so I saw no consequences. Selling dope was easy. I needed no references, work history, or uniform, and I hung out with my friends. After an hour I saw Hen and Jay-Jay, whom I found out also sold drugs at night in the Tenderloin.

Hen walked up to me and asked, "What are you doing out here so late?"

I tried to hide the fact that I was selling drugs, but as we talked, a man came up to him and asked, "You got something for ten?"

Hen barked back, "You got the whole ten?"

The man then said, "I got eight fifty."

Hen's response was, "Put the money on the ground," and the man did as he was instructed. Then Hen did something that I didn't understand at the time. He spat something out of his mouth, and the man ran after it. It wasn't until the man had walked down the street that Hen told Jay to pick up the money.

Later that night it was explained to me that if you don't make hand-to-hand transactions, it's harder to get caught. We walked up and down the Tenderloin that night and as we walked, I watched and learned a lot from them. At about twelve thirty, I was done, so I wanted to go home, but knew Tia would be sleep, or so I thought. I told myself that I would try calling the house, and if she answered, then I would stop by the booster's house and then go home. Tia answered on the first ring.

I asked her, "Tia, Mommy woke?"

She said, "No."

Then I asked, "Did they come in the room?"

"No." Tia hesitated then asked, "Tootie, you got me some clothes?"

I said, "Not yet; I need your sizes."

Excited, she gave me her sizes and we hung up.

I then went to the booster's house and picked her out three outfits and a pair of white and black Nikes. As I sneaked back in through the window, Tia immediately rushed for the bags. I turned to her and gave her ten dollars for lunch. Then I said to her "Tia, I'm leaving. I'm not coming back, but if you need me, I'll be at Peniel." With that, I turned and jumped out the window and, true to my word, I never went back—I was sixteen.

Chapter 3

The Manifestation of Corruption

As a young adult, all that I had unconsciously learned became me, and I started to manifest the corruption without thinking. There's a saying in the hood that goes, "What is in you will come out, so there's no need to try to be what you're not." In my case, that saying proved true. Everything about me at that time was corrupt because there was no longer a battle being waged: I had fully embraced the corruption. I used the hate, the frustration, and the pain as a weapon that I unleashed upon the world. These emotions held no negative connotation for me; they were delicate maidens that I caressed as I danced to the song of the streets. There was no way to stop the dance, nor did I want the song to stop. I challenged everyone and everything, I respected no one, and there was nothing I wouldn't do to further my position. Everything was on the table to be used or knocked off at my discretion. All that I had become was a direct result of my upbringing and my environment. As my environment changed, so did the principles and rules that governed it, and to learn the new principles, a teacher was needed.

Hen was our teacher, because he was what Jay-Jay and I wanted to be. Hen was a jokester, but rubbed the wrong way, he was vicious; he defended us like a male lion defends his pride. When he was with us, there was no foe we feared or couldn't defeat. So, my first two years on the streets weren't really on the streets. I spent most of the day in Pacifica at Hen's and Jay-Jay's house, and at night, I slept in their closet. At Hen's and Jay-Jay's house, "school" was always in session, and "lessons" were always being taught. If Hen wasn't teaching, then it was his mother or grandmother at the front of the class. I matured some at their house and soaked up the knowledge that helped me become the villain that I listened to on rap tapes. Although the manifestation of my corruption began at Hen and Jay-Jay's house, mixed in with the corrupt lessons were good, sound, righteous morals. These principles were being taught by their mother and grandmother, and, like the corruption, they stuck with me.

When I met their family, they lived in the Tenderloin. The family consisted of Alana, the boys, their sister Anna, and their stepdad, Tony. Hen's mother was, in my opinion, the best mother I had ever seen. Her name was Alana. She was a short, dark-skinned, slender woman of about thirty-three. Alana's character was gentle, humble, and very hardworking. She maintained the authority in the house but never raised her voice or struck anyone. If I had to describe her with one word, it would be *dedicated*. These five members of their family shared a studio, but through Alana's hard work, they moved to a two-bedroom. But a year after the move, Alana moved her family into a four-bedroom in the suburbs of San Francisco. She still wasn't satisfied, and in four years' time, she was able to buy her own house.

From Alana, I learned *even though doing what's right takes longer to benefit you, in the end hard work always pays off.* But at my age, I wasn't into waiting, so I went for the quick fix—hustling. Being an aspiring criminal, I had to be flexible: I could not always sell drugs, but I could always get a young lady to do my bidding.

For two years, I preyed upon the women in the town we lived in, manifesting many of the corrupt morals that I unconsciously learned as a child. These principles taught me to prey upon the weak, to *never trust anyone, and to use my powers to dominate and control with no compassion.* I lied to, cheated on, and manipulated the young women I dated; for me it was like a game. My experience and environment told me that was the way to manhood, and being a child, I didn't question; I just followed and hoped that no one singled me out as being different. To hide my fears, I had become a predator, seeking to benefit in every situation and from every relationship.

As a result, I became an unwelcome person at Hen and Jay-Jay's house: their mom saw straight through me and knew I was up to no good. One day we came home and I heard Alana tell Jay-Jay, "Go get Fred and tell him he has a phone call."

I ran, picked up the phone, and said, "Hello!"

To my surprise, it was my grandmother.

She said, "Tootie, it's time for you to come home. You have a family that loves and misses you."

I looked up, and Alana just walked away. To this day I don't know how either one of those women could have gotten the other's phone number, but either way I was on to new territory.

So around 1990, I ended up back in San Francisco at my grandmother's house in Hunter's Point. Hunter's Point, at that time, was sectioned off by gangs. Those gangs feuded back and forth with each other and made walking in the neighborhood dangerous. My grandparents sat me down and gave me the rules.

My grandfather said, "Tootie, be home before nine o'clock; this ain't the suburbs, and here kids are getting killed."

I said, "Okay," but in my mind I was thinking, "I can handle myself."

One bright spot about living with my grandparents was that I got to spend time with my cousin Nicole. Nicole was a pretty, light-skinned, chubby black young lady. She was my age but wasn't into anything that would have interested me. She had graduated from high school, worked, and mostly stayed at home on her off days. Outside the house, we lived in two different worlds, but in the house, we were always on the same page.

After I broke my curfew for the tenth time, my grandmother sent me to live with my auntie Sherryl. My auntie was a pretty, slender, brown-skinned woman of about 5'4" who spoke her mind, and lived in the Oakdale Housing Projects.

The Oakdale Projects were located in the back part of Hunter's Point and were a mixture of townhouses and projects, but the kids were all hood. As I walked up to the door of my auntie's house, I could see all the kids looking at me. Before I could knock, the door swung open and out jumped my three cousins. Demetri was a brown-skinned, curly-haired, young black kid. He was the oldest, and he had a mind of his own, which he never had a problem speaking. Then there was Conrad, a short dark-skinned young man of about twelve who was quiet but always watching and learning. The baby was little Bobby. He was light-skinned with red freckles and sandy red hair. These three had never played outside at Oakdale, but that was soon to change. My cousins were happy to see me for their own reasons, and I was glad to see them because of mine.

As we ran upstairs, little Bobby turned to me and asked, "Tootie, you want to play with me on my Super Nintendo?"

I responded, "Sure, why not."

As we played upstairs, we heard a car crash. We ran to the window to see what had happened and expected to see only a fender-bender; we would have never guessed that we would see a real live shootout between two carloads of heavily armed young men. *This was my first day* at *Oakdale, and I loved it.*

The Nine-Deep

I can clearly remember the moment I wanted to be a gangster: it was during a celebration for a young man from Oakdale who was gunned down. This young man had been remembered with a celebration every year since his death. This was the first time I had ever seen anything like it. All the kids, young men, and women gathered together in a spot where this man's name had been spray-painted on the wall. They turned the music on in their cars and opened the doors so the sound would carry throughout the block. The older men barbecued and passed around big bottles of Hennessey and cans of beer as everyone told stories of the young man's life. For a corrupt kid who always felt that he had something to prove, that scene excited me. As I took in the scene, I thought to myself, *"This is how I can live forever."* Not long after the party, Demetri, Conrad, and I started to hang on the upper part of the block. Once we started to hang outside, we met other boys and girls who were on the block but who weren't part of the block.

We banded together and formed our own gang, which we called the "Nine-Deep". It consisted of a bunch of ragtag youths who had little to no parental guidance. We called ourselves Nine Deep mainly because there were nine of us who started the gang— Conrad, Demetri, Chucky-B, the twins, my best friend Linin, David, Larry, and me the leader—though we added a kid we called Jala a few months later. I became the leader because there was no one around who could beat me. "The Nine", as we called ourselves, weren't from Oakdale; we just lived on the block. We spent most our days going from one gym to another playing hoops. However, we did beat up any kid we found wearing a hat that repped his hood.

I remember during the summer of 1991, the Nine was ten deep and we were headed to the Nowally-Valley gym in the upper part of the Mission district in San Francisco. As we walked, Conrad and David —the two youngest of the bunch—came to me, pointed out a boy my age, and said he had tried to beat them up at their school. My anger flared, and before I knew it, we were surrounding the young man.

He asked, "What's up?"

As I pointed to David and Conrad, I asked, "'A, you know them?"

Smiling as if he was cool with them, he said, "Yeah."

I asked, "You tried to beat on them?"

He said, "They jumped my little brother."

I called both David and Conrad to me and barked at them, "Hit him!"

Both were scared because he was twice their size and four years older than them, but I was there and I wanted them to know he was flesh, and he could be hurt. At this time, my corruption was spilling over onto the members of the Nine, and they were soaking it up like grass soaks up water after a hot summer day. As I turned to the boys, both looked as if I had told them to jump off the Golden Gate Bridge or something. So, I looked straight at David and said, "Hit him."

David gave a halfhearted swing and connected, but I wasn't satisfied, so I barked, "Hit him again, and this time really hit him!"

Once again David's hit was as if he were hitting a child, so I swung and dropped the boy to his back. Then I looked at the David and Conrad and said, "That's how you hit someone."

The boys would remember and live by this lesson, carrying their corruption to a height not even my feeble mind could have imagined. We were a tight bunch, but at age nineteen, I felt there was nothing in Oakdale for me. With the same conviction I had when I left my mom's house, I just walked away and never went back to my auntie's house. Now, I was really on the streets with nothing but my intellect and heart; but in the game, that was more than enough for me to make it.

My first task was to find a "come up" (a free "plug"), so I found AJ and asked, "Can I get a come up?"

He responded, "No!"

I asked, "Why not? I don't have a place to stay or food to eat. I need it."

See, in the game all the older men are trying to find a way out, and all the young men are trying to get in. AJ knew what I didn't. He had seen the good, the bad, and the ugly about the streets, and he didn't want to start me on my way to hell.

He pulled me to the side and said, "Go home!"

I replied, "If you don't want to help that's cool, but I'm not going home!"

I walked off mad because I could not see into the distant future that AJ dreaded I would encounter. I got my come up money by snatching a purse. I never gave any thought if the woman was a mother whose money was for her rent or food for her kids. I had completely lost my conscience, and my feelings were nonexistent, but it would get worse.

Back in the Tenderloin, I made a name for myself; my corrupt morals were now manifesting themselves in my interactions with others, and the people were now recognizing me. In an environment where everyone has "heart" (toughness), mine shined. One day, a friend and I were hanging in front of a store with three very pretty young ladies. Three men from Sunnydale (a section of San Francisco) named J.T., Kofi, and Joe parked their car and also stood in front of the store. J.T., the oldest and leader of the men, said to one of the girls, "Can I get your number?"

She responded, "I got a man."

I saw that the girl wasn't interested in him, so as they roughhoused to get the girls' attention, I slid in and got the phone number. As we talked, J.T. came up behind me and hit me on the back of the head. Not knowing what was happening, I stumbled into the store, but when I turned around and saw that it was him who hit me, my rage grew. I grabbed a bottle on the counter but before I could throw it, J.T. said, "Throw it, but how you gon' get out?" It became a test of heart.

I slammed the bottle back on the counter and said, "I'm gon' walk out!"

I then walked straight for him, and as I passed him, once more he hit me in the back of the head. Not knowing if any of them had a gun or not, I ran around the corner and picked up my friend, and we went to go get my gun to even my odds since it was three against one. It was a short four blocks to the hotel where the gun was stashed, but it felt more like ten miles. After picking up the gun, we rushed backed to the store, and when we arrived, they were still there. When I turned the corner and saw them, murder was on my mind, but before I could get close enough to shoot him, they turned around and saw me. As J.T. pointed towards the gun, he asked, "What you gon' do with that?"

I barked back, "Nothing! You a man I'm a man—we gon' fight! The gun is to make sure that no one jumps in."

J.T. was what we called "penitentiary built," thick with muscles at thirty-six years old, standing 5'11" and weighing 210 lbs. He had been in the streets since he was a boy. I, on the other hand, was 5'9", 175 lbs., and just coming out of boyhood, but like the young lion that challenges the old leader, I stood ready to attack. I let off the first five blows; these were usually my knockout punches, but as they landed he neither fell nor moved. Instead, the blows instantly caused blood to flow from his nose and mouth, and he just shook it off. Then he looked me right in my eyes and said, "I'm gon' hurt you!"

At that point all the anger I felt left me, and my safety was all I thought about. I didn't run or back down, but I did make sure that when I hit him, I did it fast and got away even faster. I didn't knock him out or down, but everyone there saw when it came to fighting I could handle myself. So my reputation grew, and before my twentieth birthday, I had two workers, a woman who brought in ten thousand every other week and a rep.

My woman was my best friend. She kept me sane in a world built on insanity, and she allowed me to love. Her name was Tunisia Mannings.

Tunisia was a bright young lady from the suburbs of Oakland, California. She was uncorrupted by the environment around us. Tunisia was a chubby dark-skinned young lady who was about eighteen years old, very pretty, and self-willed. I watched Tunisia from afar and liked the way she handled herself.

Nisi's stepdad, Tim, was to the Tenderloin what Jason of the *Friday the Thirteenth* movies was—big and scary. Tim was 5'10" and weighed 200 lbs. He wore his hair long and uncombed. He had a scar in the middle of his forehead, which made him look like a red-eyed demon when he smoked weed. He robbed, beat, and shot anyone who challenged him, so he was someone nobody messed with. No one could talk to Nisi unless he approved, and he approved of no one. One day while Tim was gone, Nisi got jacked (stopped and searched) by the police and had to eat a fifty-rock (fifty dollars' worth) of dope. She was scared and none of her people were around, so I stepped up and took her with me.

We ended up in a Taco Bell on Market Street, and after I calmed her nerves, we talked. In the space of about six hours we opened up our hearts to each other, telling of things that neither one of us had ever told anyone else. When we walked into that Taco Bell, we were strangers, but when we left, we were connected by our souls. When Tim found us, he told her, "Go get in the car," and as she ran off, he just turned my way and frowned, but two weeks later we were together again and this time it was for good. Nisi and I hustled together every night for forty-five days. We slept in the same bed, but never touched each other.

One day, she asked me, "Fred, my grandparents used to tell me about something they called a courtship—is that what we're doing?"

I said, "No, we're just taking our time." The truth was I was cautious because of Tim.

On the forty-sixth day, Nisi said, "Fred, we doing it tonight!"

I said, "What?"

She responded, "You heard me!"

So, that night we got the E&J Brandy and had planned to get the weed, but forgot. When we remembered we didn't have the weed, I said, "Baby, I'll be right back. Get ready."

I went to jail that night and didn't see her again for three months. Jail did me good, because I now knew I could handle doing the time. Also, while I was locked up I got physically bigger, which helped me in the streets.

At twenty-two I was a terror, standing 5'9" and tipping the scales at a whopping 185 lbs. of muscle. I felt unstoppable. I returned to Oakdale with money, respect, and a rep. The young men welcomed me back. The name Freddy-Gz (pronounced "Geez") was given to me by a girl, and it stuck. In my opinion, this nickname aided in my downfall, because it became known throughout the city. At that time, I no longer sold drugs, but I started to rob drug dealers and dice games—which in itself is crazy, but the seeds of corruption were now in full bloom. Despite this, in the garden of my life, among the thorns, thistles, and weeds of my character were the most beautiful flowers. These flowers were the women that I surrounded myself with, which during that time were numerous.

The most influential flower in my life during that time was Dawn. Dawn was a slender, beautiful, loving, compassionate, and generous white girl from my past. During my high school years, she was one of Hen's girls, but I always liked her.

One day I got a call from Hen's mother.

"Hello, Fred, it's Alana. Henry is in jail and I was wondering if you will go with Dawn to see him and put money on his books?"

I said, "Yeah, just give her my number and tell her to call me."

My first thoughts were of Hen, because what his mother didn't know was I already knew where he was. I was with him when he got caught—I just got away. When I met up with Dawn, I didn't expect to hook up with her, but as I looked into her innocent face, I succumbed to my lust.

It took some time to win Dawn over, but I was up for the challenge, and in the summer of '96 we consummated our relationship. For me, it was nothing special, just sex, but for her it became so much more. After Dawn and I had sex, I forgot all about her until she called me four weeks later. I was at another female friend's house asleep, and when my phone rang, the lady answered it. I was awakened to the sound of her saying, "Fred, it's a woman on the phone saying she's pregnant, and it's yours."

I rolled over and said, "Give me my phone." I placed the phone to my face and said, "Hello."

It was Dawn. I listened as she shouted at me, "Fred, I'm pregnant!"

I calmly responded," Who's the father?"

Dawn got really quiet and then said, "Fred, it's yours."

I said, "Stop playing with me!" I then hung up the phone, threw it on the chair, and tried to go back to sleep, but the young lady I was with at the time wouldn't let me.

She said, "Until you go see if that's your baby, I'm not messing with you." I got up and left, but all day I was haunted by the thought that it may be true—I didn't use protection that night.

Early the next morning, I was on my way to Dawn's house. Dawn and I started a relationship, and I moved in with her. My "extracurricular activities" didn't change. I continued doing drugs and sleeping with every woman I could manipulate into bed. Dawn was sensitive and very loving, but her loyalty and devotion was wasted on me. I wasn't into love, nor did I feel for others. My only concern at that time was to benefit myself, so to me, Dawn was a tool to be used.

Dawn tried her best to keep her family together for the first few months, but by her eighth month, she was telling me the only reason she was still with me was because of the emotions that came with the pregnancy. I took that to mean once the baby came, she would be gone. We patiently waited for her to go into labor for our own reasons. Both of us wanted me to be there at the birth of our child, but our hopes would be dashed by my stupidity. Five months into Dawn's pregnancy, another woman I was having sex with told me that I was the father of her unborn child. Her name was Debra, and although she wasn't my "main chick" at the time, she would become my wife in the near future.

For the entire time during both of these pregnancies, my habits and my actions were unchanged. When one accepts the corruption, he or she accepts all that comes with it, and in my case that meant doing drugs. There had always been drugs around me, but I had never taken them. Watching how drugs took control of my parents and the misery it caused me and Tia made me hate them, but by this time, all those memories were gone and I chose to taste the forbidden fruit of cocaine. I was snorting cocaine, smoking weed, drinking alcohol, and robbing drug dealers and dice games every night. Cocaine made me feel as if I were invincible. It gave me that edge that propelled me to even more daring crimes.

During 1996, I started to hang out and commit robberies with an older man from Oakdale named Jonathan. "Jon" was a stocky dark-skinned black man who stood about 5'5" and who never had a problem putting in work. Jon loved the fact that he had a youngster who didn't mind holding the pistol and was willing to rob anyone at the drop of a hat. We spent money all day and went to the strip clubs at night. By 2:30 AM, we would be looking to make our money back out of the pockets of the drug dealers of Tenderloin. One night after we left the strip club drunk and headed for the Tenderloin, we came upon two police officers sitting in their car. Being the arrogant and disrespectful child that I was, I pulled up on the side of them and asked sarcastically, "'Ey, y'all gon' be in that parking space for long?"

The cop driving gave me a stern face and said, "Get the hell out of here."

Driving off we laughed as I said, "Fuck 'em." Little did I know I would be at the mercy of those same cops just a few minutes later. We drove around the block and spotted some young men and women hanging out by a car, so we parked, loaded the gun, and got out. As we walked up on the crowd I spotted a girl I knew, so I said, "What's up, pretty girl?"

She smiled and said, "Nothing; what's up wit' you? You wit' me tonight?"

I said, "'Ey, come walk with me." As we walked I asked, "Pretty girl, how well do you know those other guys?"

She said, "I really don't know them, they just stopped us so we could smoke with them."

I then asked, "Have they been making sales?"

She responded with, "Hell, yeah, they ain't stop. It's juking (meaning that money was coming through fast) out here."

Before we could pull out our gun, the cops showed up and told everyone to get against the wall. Jon motioned to me to run because I had the gun, but I stayed. As the police started to frisk me, I turned and let off two heavy-fisted blows that dropped the cop to the ground, and then I ran off. As I jumped a fence that led to a park, the cop opened fire. It was only by the grace of God that I didn't get hit that night—before the shots rang out, I had accidently fallen on my face as the bullets flew over my head. Since I was drunk and had been smoking weed and cigars, I had no wind and could not run another step. I hid the gun, ran to the back of the park, and fell out. I was caught that night, and although I was guilty they could not find the gun, so I was only charged with assault on a police officer and evading capture, but I was only held on a probation violation. Two months later, I was released on bail. Even though I had escaped with my life, my corruption would keep me in situations that would constantly endanger my life.

Chapter 4

The Inevitable Consequence of my Actions

The Fall

Many times, I cheated death. To stay safe, I was no longer able to take direct routes to any of my destinations. By this time, my enemies were scattered throughout the city and were constantly shooting at me. Frequently during this period, it was only by the grace of God that I got away, but I didn't heed the warnings.

One day as I finished my bundle of dope, I decided to smoke some weed to celebrate my day's sales. After the blunt was done, I clearly remember looking to the right and no one was there. Then I looked to the left and no one was there as well, but as I turned back to the right, a young man stood there and asked, "You got a twenty shot (a twenty-dollar piece of dope)?" By this time, the weed had me physically and mentally slow, so I didn't realize that I was about to be robbed.

I responded back, "All I got is a crumb sack."

The young man then said, "You think I'm playing!" He pulled out a .45 automatic pistol, so I dug in my left pocket and came out with a bag of crumbs and the twenty dollars I had just made but bypassed the three thousand in my right pocket. At this, the young man became angry and hit me.

Without a thought, my reflexes kicked in, and before I knew it I swung and knocked him to the ground. As a bear does before it attacks, I now stood over him ready to unleash my fury. My aggression moved me, so I forgot he had a gun. I started for him, but he jumped up and cocked the gun, pointed it at me, and pulled the trigger. To both our surprise, the gun didn't fire.

At the exact same time, we looked down at the gun to see a bullet sticking out its side. The gun had jammed; I knew it wouldn't fire, so I started at him again, but after two steps, the bullet popped out. We both froze, and together we watched as the bullet slowly fell to the ground. Once the bullet hit the concrete, we looked up at each other, but before he could aim, I ran into the street and got away. At the time my actions were the right ones for the situation, but I now realize this only showed the self-destructive way of life I had embraced.

My reputation, ego, and drug habit grew to the extreme. I was feared by the people around me but was in a daze most of the time due to the drugs. To be feared was my motivation in every act I performed. I just didn't understand that gaining the object of my desires would hasten my demise. My pride made me vulnerable because I took no precautions to protect myself from the enemies I had amassed while on my destructive, terror-filled mission of becoming someone to be feared. I believed the cocaine-induced hype that I was invincible and couldn't be hurt. All reality and common sense had eluded me. Those who are feared lose the common sense to know they can be hurt.

On August 3, 1997, I was introduced to not only my vulnerability but also my mortality. That day started for me like every other day. I awoke to a beautiful woman, money in my pocket, and plans to go to the city after I showered. I arrived in the city around one o'clock and went straight to work—by work, I mean I made my rounds and picked up the money from my workers in the streets.

At about three o'clock, I made my way to Oakdale where I hooked up with a man called "Tray". Tray was older than me and had been doing dirt (committing crimes) in the hood since he was a child. He was a tall, slim, young man with corn rolls in his hair and a slang that sounded like he was always up to something. He said, "Gz, I have a quarter of powder—what's up!"

I yelled back, "It's all good!" I then jumped out of my car and into his.

We rode through Hunter's Point snorting and hollering at women and young girls. At about six o'clock we made our way to the Sunnydale Housing Projects, where Tray's son's mother lived. She was a beautiful dark-skinned woman of about twenty-three. Her skin was very smooth and her body type was a perfect mixture of "thick" and slender that fit her personality to a tee. While in her house, we ate food and drank alcohol for an hour. Every time Tray would be in another room, his son's mom would flirt with me. I didn't know if it was the drugs or if what I believed was happening was really happening. Before we left I asked her, "Hey, can I get yo' number?"

She said, "You have to ask Tray."

When I asked him, he said, "Man, that's my baby's momma. It ain't cool."

I backed off, but the damage was done. All the way back he was quiet, until we ran out of powder. Tray looked over at me and said, "I got to go to my house."

I said, "Let's go."

While waiting for Tray, I spotted a young man selling dope, and as I watched he must have made fifteen to twenty sales. My mind instantly started working, and in a split second, I decided to rob him. Once Tray got back in the car, I said, "Tray, I'm through—drop me off at my car."

Sitting in my car, I realized I didn't have my gun with me so I could rob the young man, but I knew I could use someone else's from the block. I called my "little brother" from The Nine and said, "David, I need a gun."

He responded, "All I have is a .357 Magnum and it's big, Gz."

"I'll be there in two minutes, so come outside," As I drove up, I could see that David was already outside. When he recognized me, he ran to the car.

I asked him, "Is it loaded?"

He said, "Yeah—what's up? Who you gon' hit?"

I responded, "No one, I just need to get some money."

Then David said, "Gz, take me with you."

I was greedy in those days, and because I didn't want to split the money, I said, "No."

I then drove off to carry out my plans. I parked one block away from where I saw the young man hustling, checked the gun for bullets, and then stepped out the door into darkness.

As I started for the 89th block of Humphrey Avenue, my thinking was clear, my gun was loaded, and my resolve was unshaken. When I came up out of the staircase, I put my hood on and clenched the .357 Magnum in my pocket. As soon as the young man saw me, he ran for his house. By this time, I was set on getting what I had come for, and him running in the house didn't deter me. I saw the door he entered, but what I didn't see was that on the other side of that door were heavily armed men who were ready to kill. Unaware of this fact, I began to bang on the door, and after some time a man appeared. "What's up?" He said.

"You got something for ten?" I asked. He stuck his hand in his pocket and pulled out a small piece of dope, and as he looked down, I stuck my gun in his belly and said, "Break yo' self!"

As a "jacker" (armed robber), you are taught that the most dangerous thing when robbing is the victim's hands because a weapon in them could kill you. Therefore, I went for the hand I could not see, but I slipped as I stepped up. He capitalized on my mistake by taking his gun out, placing it on my chest, and letting it loose. I didn't hear the sound of the gun going off, nor did I feel the bullet rip through my flesh or myself falling to the ground, but all these things took place. What I do remember is the darkness of death and the coldness of that night.

I sat in darkness for I don't know how long, but just as quickly as the darkness had engulfed me I was back in my body. When my eyes opened, I was sitting on the ground with my legs stretched out in front of me and my back straight up. My first thoughts were: *"He hit me"*, and then the cold reality: *"I'm 'bout to die on the Hump."* That night was a defining moment in my life— up until *th*at incident, time was set on, filled with, and controlled by evil, which led to pride, greed, and selfishness. The principles I learned as a child, internalized as youth, and manifested as a young adult had laid the foundation for my death.

The aftermath, and the struggle to live

Up until the incident, I had not known fear or mental and physical pain, but as time passed they became my greatest allies. My granddad once told me that a man is not a man unless he is tested through adversity. My test would push me to the brink of destruction and show me what I was really made of. Anger, frustration, and hate were the mediums that helped nourish the corruption I dealt with. However, in order to grow, I would have to learn to let these emotions go and through pain and fear be transformed into the man my parents wanted me to be. At that time, I thought that losing my legs was the worst thing that could have happened to me. But in the Spirit realm, I would come to understand that it was the best thing for me. That night in August was a culmination of a past filled with corruption, as well as a life driven by violence, hate, and a lack of resources. I would later regret who I had become; I would never forget the lessons I learned as a result of that experience. The reality my experience would create for me would be devastating, but at the

time of its dawning, I responded as I had always done—
with anger.

My eyes opened to the reality that I couldn't
walk, but my anger had carried me to a place that most
would think was unthinkable. My gun lay beside me as I
yelled at the front door of the assailant. "I have two
thousand dollars on me, come get it! Open the door, you
coward! If I die I'm gon' kill you!"

As I was yelling, a woman from another
apartment opened her door and asked, "Is it anything I
can do for you?"

I responded, "Yeah, it would be good if you
could come get this gun from me."

She replied, "I can't do that, baby, but I'll call the
ambulance for you."

I said, "Thank you—that's good."

"Hang in there, baby. They'll be here in a
minute," She answered.

All I could do while I lay there was think about
the warrant for my arrest and what to do with the gun. I
knew if I were caught with the gun, it would be a new
case, so I decided to throw it in the bushes—but I missed
and it landed on the stairs. It was as if nothing was going
to go right that night. The first to arrive were the police.

I lay there for about ten minutes with a white cop kneeling over me, yelling, "You gon' make it—hang in there! They're on their way! Hang in there. I'll be here with you! I won't leave you!"

If I wasn't shot and worried about going to jail after I got out the hospital, I would have told him to get the hell out my face with all that yelling. Instead of pushing him away, I drew him closer and played into his fantasy and started to yell over and over again, "I took one of their guns. I took one of their guns."

The more I yelled, I could hear the police say to each other, "He must be in shock!"

I knew that I wasn't in shock, but *even at the point of death, I was still trying to manipulate the people around me.* The roots of corruption had sprouted deep into my character; this was evident by the fruits of unrighteousness I presented to the world. The ambulance came about twenty minutes after the police, and medics began to work on me.

They ripped off my shirt and sweater as one of the technicians asked me, "Do you know your name, and what city are you in?"

I stated, "My name is Traivonne, and we are in San Francisco."

He then asked, "What happened, and whose gun did we pass as we came down the stairs?"

I said, "They tried to rob me, and I took one of their guns."

By this time in my life, a lie rolled off my lips like the truth and people bought it as if it were true, so they didn't question me further.

All was going just as I planned until I entered into the ambulance, and suddenly it took a turn for the worst. Out of nowhere, I felt the worst pain I had ever felt in my entire young life. It was the same prickling sensation you feel when you try to move after your legs have fallen asleep. The sensation felt like millions of pins and needles in my legs pushing to burst out. During the whole ride, I yelled and screamed for pain meds. The technician just kept repeating, "We can't. It will make it hard for the doctor to treat you, but they'll give you something when we get there."

Once in the operating room, the doctors and nurses went about the task of hooking me to machines that would monitor my vital signs. I continued to ask for meds but they kept saying, "You have to wait," so I began to rip the cords that they had placed on my body off.

The nurses and doctors tried to restrain me, but because of the pain I was unusually strong. They grabbed my arms and yelled, "Stop! You need these on!"

I just kept screaming, "I need pain meds! I can't take it! The pain is too much!"

The next thing I remember, I was in the recovery room. As I opened my eyes, I could see Dawn sitting beside my bed. For the next two weeks I slept, but I periodically opened my eyes to see different members of my family standing over me. As I entered the third week of my recuperation, I opened my eyes for good. It wasn't until the doctors thought I was mentally and physically ready to handle the news of my condition that they gathered my family and had the dreaded meeting.

My dad, brothers, sisters, and I sat in a conference room in the hospital awaiting the news from the doctors concerning my future prognosis. As the doctors entered the room, an ominous feeling settled upon the room. There was no smiling or horse-playing like before. Each member of the family stared intently at the doctors and waited to hear what the future held for me. With stern faces, the doctors entered the room and with only a few words they took my reason to live away.

As easily as one would greet a stranger, the doctors looked me in the face and said, "You will never be able to walk again."

I didn't believe it and responded, "You lying! I can feel my legs!"

The doctors just asked, "Can you please move your toes for us?"

With all my might I tried to move them, but my toes didn't move. I was devastated.

I tried to hold it together because I didn't want to show any weakness. My brothers and sisters always looked to me to be the sword that upheld them and their causes, so I felt I had to be strong. However, mentally I was broken and lost. Every night after everyone left, I would sit up and cry for hours. Even though I didn't believe in God or have a personal relationship with him, I stayed up late every night asking him, "Why me?"

I was in the hospital for three months. The first month I was in and out of consciousness, but the last two I was fully awake. The last two months I learned how to live without the use my legs. I had wheelchair training and bowel training, and they taught me how to cook and care for my young son. The therapists who tended to me were kind and understanding, but they didn't understand me. John, one of my therapists, was a tall, slender white man with long blonde hair that he usually wore in a ponytail. He was kind and motivating, and he helped me believe my life wasn't over but was just now starting.

One day while Dawn and my son were there, John asked me a question that rocked my world for fifteen years. I had entered the workout room, and I saw John there already talking to Dawn. As they turned around and saw me, John asked, "Fred, where do you go from here? God has given you another chance at life, don't waste it."

I responded, "I don't know."

He said, "You have a beautiful family right here that is willing to support you; most young men that come through here don't."

"What can I do? I don't have my legs!" I yelled. I looked at Dawn as if she were the enemy and turned and rolled out.

I couldn't see hope because I was filled with so much despair. However, I never stopped thinking about that question. I sat in that room looking at my young son sitting on the lap of his loving and dedicated mother, and I wanted to change, but all I knew was depravity. I had never done the right thing, and I didn't want to. I feared the change they were asking me to make. I thought if I were to leave the gang, what would my people say? Who will protect me from my enemies, or help me when I needed financial support? The unknown is a scary place, even for someone who thought they feared nothing. So, once I was out of the hospital, I fell back to what I knew. I realized I couldn't be the man I had been before, but I also knew I still held power in the community, and I intended to wield it.

Even while I was in the hospital, I stayed in touch with the hood. Dawn would often come up to the hospital after the therapist left, and she would take me out. On our excursions I drank and smoked weed and cigars; in a way, it made me feel normal again. Dawn didn't like for me to leave, but she was my lady, and as such, she stayed in her place. I believe she did this to show me her support and love. Now that I think about it, those times must have been extremely hard for her-- seeing me in that environment acting like a thug and then going back to the hospital and needing her to clean me up after I had a bowel movement. There were many men in the hood who wanted to take care of the dude who shot me, but I had other worries that clouded my mind.

One of the most important things I needed to know was: will I still be able to have sex? The doctors could not tell me if it would be possible or not. They just kept telling me that we would have to wait until the swelling in my spine subsided. But I couldn't wait, so while Dawn and I were alone in the room, I asked her to come get on top of me. She was more than willing, and before I knew it we were hugging, kissing, and touching each other in the bed. I was worked up, but my nature didn't rise. It could have been humiliating if I were with any other woman, but Dawn had a compassionate spirit; she was so encouraging, loving, and understanding that she brought me out of my sorrow.

As she rolled off me she said, "Fred, it's not a big deal. You just had major surgery and your spine is still swollen. It will come—just be patient."

I asked her, "What if it don't work for me ever again? How can I be a man? How can I keep you if I can't please you?

She responded with, "Fred, you still have your fingers and tongue; you better learn how to work them." I looked at her and we busted up laughing. She always knew how to change my moods.

For the last two months I was in the hospital, Dawn was there every night after work. She never complained or refused me anything. She worked eight hours a day, five days a week, took care of our son, and took care of me. I could see she was drained, but I needed her, and she knew it. So, she put her personal life to the side to be with me. I was angry and depressed, so I took out my frustrations on her, and she took it. Life had changed for me in one second, and I regretted that second every day I was in the hospital.

The counselors of the hospital made sure I signed up for SSI before I was discharged. This was supposed to be a help, but I only qualified for $832.00 a month, which was beyond frustrating because that was what I made in just two hours hustling. Until John and Dawn helped me to leave the past in its place and start to look to the future, my every thought was of the streets. I tried not to think of life outside the hospital, but I soon came face to face with the beauty I had previously overlooked about life.

One day, John came into the workout room where I was lifting weights and asked, "Fred, you want to go outside for a while?"

I looked up and asked, "You for real?" This was the first time I was able to see sunshine since being admitted.

He said, "Yeah."

I responded, "Yeah, I want to go, but where we going?"

John said, "Fred, I want to show you something, but you're going have to wait to see it."

I said, "All right, let's go."

The anticipation was killing me. I was excited, worried, and ready; after all, I had been confined to the ward for three months. After lunch, John stuck his head in my room and asked, "Fred, you ready?

I said, "Yeah."

John's big surprise was exactly what I needed. He took me across the street from the hospital to Golden Gate Park. He chose the park because it was the time of year when flowers were in full bloom, which signifies new life. We entered the park on the north side, where everywhere I looked there were the most vibrant colors.

It was as if I had never seen a flower before. I noticed that the yellows of the flowers were like the shining of the noonday sun. The ground all around me was covered with a carpet of the darkest green grass that I had ever seen. I saw flowers that were as blue as the ocean. The purple flowers reminded me of the robes worn by Catholic priests. The colors were so deep and dark that I got lost in them. The colors that stood out the most were the bright ones like the orange in the lilies, the green of the orchids, the white with a reddish center of the red heart rose of Sharon flowers, and my favorite the Big Bang Tickseed flowers that were red with an orange center. The atmosphere was one of beauty, peace, and life. It totally took over my being. It felt like the world was new, and I was experiencing things that I had ignored before the incident, but at the time, I didn't realize the significance of that experience. I would later recognize it as my rebirth into the world. All around me there were blessings, but because of my situation, I didn't notice them. Despite this rebirth, I left the hospital exactly three and a half months after the incident with a chip on my shoulder and a bad attitude.

Freedom from the confines of the hospital brought new challenges to my life. In the hospital, the ground was a level and of a smooth tile that was very easy for me to roll on. In contrast, the concrete of the outdoors was unleveled, rough, and very hard for me to navigate. I hated for people to walk behind me and push, so I stayed in the house most of the time. It pained me to see people walking, which caused me to develop a hatred for those who were upright. I resented Dawn for having a life and options when it came to relationships. Instead of loving her for sticking by me, I clung to other women, which pushed her away. I was afraid to be alone and feared the thought that I would be in this condition for the rest of my life. The only things that brought me comfort were 2Pac CDs and E&J Brandy. I use to think being trapped in prison would be one of the worst things that could happen to me, but being trapped in the prison of my mind was a far greater punishment than I could have ever imagined.

They say thought is the wine that intoxicates intelligent people, but for me it was the source of my madness. Each night, I would dream of being back on the block, but every morning I awakened to the reality that I would never be there again in the same capacity. That thought above all others hurt the most. I loved being on the block selling dope, packing pistols, and shining at the many different clubs I frequented, and despite the fact that I was in a wheelchair, my thoughts were of the block. The second thought that tormented me was how I could keep the women in my life if I could not perform sexually. Dawn was comforting and very supportive, but

I kept thinking it was only a matter of time before she left me. It's funny, I mind-tripped so hard that I actually caused what I feared to happen. Because I feared Dawn would leave, I kept a backup woman around. Her name was Debra, and she had claimed I was the father of her unborn child. I spent time with both women, and although Debra knew of Dawn, Dawn knew nothing of Debra.

The Birth of Love

I thought I was going to have both women, but my cheating blew up in my face, and I was confronted by both of them. At the time, I was living with my oldest sister Shawn in Oakland, California. Shawn had just gotten clean of drugs and was trying to live right. Shawn couldn't stand the thought that one day Dawn would show up while Debra was there, and she wouldn't know what to say. Although she had never told me how she felt or asked me to tell Debra not to come by, she took it upon herself to "fix my life," and she told Dawn about Debra.

I remember it was at the end of 1997 on a beautiful Tuesday morning when Debra called me and said, "Fred, Dawn called me last night."

I said, "How she get yo' number?"

Debra asked, "Fred, you didn't give it to her?"

I said, "No."

Then she said, "Fred, she wants me to meet her at Shawn's house later tonight after she gets off work."

My response was, "Why? You bet' not show up. I mean it, Debra."

She then told me, "Fred, I'm already on my way to Shawn's house."

I hung up mad and went to get dressed.

The whole time that I was picking out my clothes and shoes, I was thinking of how she could've gotten Debra's phone number. At first, I thought Dawn got the number from our phone bill, but we didn't have a shared line and my bill went to Shawn's house. Then I thought maybe Debra called her and was just lying to me by saying Dawn initiated the contact, but I knew that Debra wouldn't do anything to hurt me. I blamed friend and foe alike for this breach in my secrecy. The most obvious answer was Shawn gave it to her, but this was one thought that never crossed my mind. I fully trusted my sister and believed that she had my best interest at heart, so her betrayal hurt more than anything else up to that date. I was caught between a rock and a hard place, but I reasoned I could make Debra go home—or so I thought.

Debra arrived a little after I was dressed, and I immediately said, "Debra, you got to go back home."

Her response was, "No—I'm staying, Fred."

I asked, "Why do you want to see her? What you think gon' happen?"

Debra said, "Fred, you gon' have to choose today. Is you gon' be with me or her?"

For the first time in our relationship of four years, Debra would not listen to me. She had made up her mind, and she was sticking to it. I tried to get her to go home for two reasons: the first was I didn't want them to meet for my own selfish reasons, but the second was for her. If they pushed me to choose, I knew I would pick Dawn—not because I felt for her more, but because I didn't want to be separated from my son. I knew this would hurt Debra more than cheating on her could have ever done. As I was urging Debra to leave, I didn't notice that Shawn had asked me to give her fifty cents for the phone until it was too late. Twenty minutes after Shawn's phone call, Dawn came bursting through the door wearing a black beanie cap, black clothes, and a look that said, "I'm ready for war."

Dawn asked, "What's up, Fred?"

I said, "Nothing," but I knew I was finally caught. Debra stood there quiet and never said a word, but Dawn vocalized her disapproval very loudly.

Shawn then said, "Y'all got to take that outside."

So, Dawn asked, "Fred, can we go in the backyard and talk about this?"

I responded, "Yeah, let's go."

Once we entered the backyard, both women wanted me to make a choice. All I could do was laugh. I was caught, and there was nothing I could do or say to make the situation better. My laughter didn't bother Debra, but Dawn felt disrespected, and she hit me in the chest and said, "Ain't nothing funny, Fred."

Shawn saw it and stepped in, saying, "That ain't cool, Dawn; don't touch him. Y'all can talk it out, but all that hitting ain't going down."

So, I sat there with a woman on either side of me-- both mad, both wanting me, and both waiting for my answer. After a few minutes, I knew I couldn't get out of this situation without making a choice, so I chose Dawn. I reasoned that I knew Dawn's son was mine, but I wasn't sure of Debra's child, so I picked the sure thing. After I gave my answer to the question of who I would be with, Dawn immediately said, "Let's go."

We jumped into her car and sped away, leaving Debra at Shawn's house. The only problem was that Dawn had to go back to work. Although I chose Dawn, she was still upset. She knew she could not trust me. As we pulled up to her job, she said, "Fred, you have to stay in the car. I'll leave you the keys so you can listen to the radio, but I'm taking your wheels to the chair."

I sat in that car for six and a half hours waiting for her to get off work. By the time she came back, my legs were hurting so bad that all I wanted to do was lie down. At the time, I never looked at the experience of Debra, Dawn, and myself through the eyes of the women, but today I can see the pain they went through.

I was almost helpless and was dependent on others for physical, mental, and emotional support, but I was so ungrateful, deceitful, and downright disrespectful of others' feelings. As a thug, I paid no attention to others' feelings or emotions. I was absorbed in only what mattered to me. I hurt the people around me by default. I did not see the pain I was causing others by the choices I made. I never realized that creating a reality that only suited me would doom me to a life of loneliness and regret. Shawn's decision to tell Dawn didn't just hurt the relationship between Dawn and me. It also placed a rift between Shawn and me. I thought Dawn was the better choice at the time because she was motivated, compassionate, and very supportive.

But in those days, I wasn't looking for a supportive woman. I was looking for an obedient woman. I was looking for a woman who had time to buy my weed, I was looking for a woman who would shun her responsibilities to lay up with me, and I was looking for a woman who would accept the abuse I would put her through because of my pain. Dawn was not that woman, nor did I want to fashion her into that woman, so three weeks later, after seeing Debra on the block, I decided to walk away from Dawn and into the arms of Debra.

For a disrespectful, hateful, and deceitful man, Debra was like a dream come true, because she loved so hard that she didn't care. I guess it was because Debra had never known what it meant to be loved by a man, so she believed that having a baby, taking abuse, and doing what she was told would lead to me loving her. Thinking back, I'm ashamed of the way I treated her and the things I had her doing. During those times, my legs were always in pain, and I found out that a mixture of weed and Tylenol with codeine would stop the pain. Many late nights I sent Debra out to the streets to search for these things, and she went without complaint. I never had a thought for her safety or well-being; my consideration was only for whether her search would be successful or not. In the life I was living, having a loyal woman who would move heaven or hell to obey me was needed more than my right arm. In many ways, Debra became the legs I didn't have and the woman who would show me how to love.

When Debra and I moved back to San Francisco and into our new apartment together in the fall of 1998, two opposing forces met. On one hand, Debra was uneducated, homely, and very loving, and on the other hand, I was quick thinking, a man of the streets, and filled with hate. I projected all the hate I could upon her, not because I hated her but because that was all I had to give at that time. Still, Debra never complained, nor did she ever form her mouth to tell me no or stop about anything I did or asked her to do. Some may say she was stupid or weak, but today I see she was stronger than I had ever been. She had given up her life to care for me, and I showed her no appreciation. Anyone can hang in there while love is flowing—that takes no strength—but to keep loving when all you receive is hate, disrespect, and pain takes a strength that can only come through real love, and Debra had just that kind of love.

In the house along with Debra and I were our kids. Anita was our oldest, and although she was Debra's child, I fell in love with her love for me. From the outset, Anita and I connected because I was searching for a child to take care of, and she was looking for a dad. Anita stuck by my side in the house and helped her mom to care for me. Our next child was my son Traivonne. He was the child I had with Dawn, and he was in my house most of the time because Dawn had to work. Vonne and I had our own relationship that the other kids couldn't understand, but no one felt as if they didn't matter. When I looked at Vonne, I saw myself as a child. He was well mannered, helpful, and very loving. He often fought with the other kids because he wanted me all to himself.

Vonne looked up to me, and although I was still thugging, I tried to teach him what was right. I just didn't understand that kids rarely listen to what parents say, but they watch what they do and imitate that. Our youngest child was Jaishawn. He was also Debra's child, but I loved him as my own. In the house, no one knew what I used to do in my life. No one knew of the money that passed through my hands as a thug or the many cars I drove while I was in the streets, but they loved me because I was a dad, a husband, and a brother.

As the illumination of light changes the blackness of a dark room, so did love change the hate that saturated me. It wasn't my intention to change, nor did I see the transformation coming, but slowly the people in the house converted me into a new man. Although hate was the dominant emotion inside of me, the love that began to form was stronger. Through the eyes of my kids, I saw a man who loved. The kids always wanted to be around me, and they loved for me to play with them. I could not be hateful to the kids or Debra's younger sisters, but the feelings I displayed towards them I wouldn't say were love. I recognized their love for me every day but didn't know how to reciprocate it.

Debra was a virtuous woman. She worked, hustled, cooked, cleaned, cared for the kids, and catered to me as if she were my personal attendant. I started to recognize her sacrifice three years after we were married and moved in together. I began to feel for her in a way I had never felt for any other person except my mom. I can still recall the first time I realized I was in love with her.

We were high on ecstasy and had been making love all night, but I had not gotten a release. I wanted to keep going, but she was tired and her vagina was hurting, so she wanted to go to sleep. I was horny and didn't want to stop, so I got up, went into the kitchen, and called a female friend named Carla and asked, "Carla, can I come over?"

She asked, "Why, what's up?"

My response was, "You know what I want—don't play."

She laughed and said, "It's good; come over. I'll be here."

I hung up the phone with the intention of going over to her house to have sex, but as I turned and looked at Debra lying in bed, I realized I only wanted to have sex with her. I sat there steaming, asking myself, "Why do I feel this way?" I could've had what I wanted, but I literally couldn't bring myself to do it. The thought came to me: *You can't do it because you love her.* My mouth dropped open, and I instantly got mad as I sat there staring at her. Up until that moment, I had always done whatever I wanted to with no care for others, but now I was worrying about how she would feel, and I hated it. I hated putting someone above my own desires, but I could not help it. Love had carried me away, and like the wind, I could not see where it came from or where it was going.

My inability to comprehend the emotions I was feeling and my desire to be selfish caused me to resist the feelings of love that were infiltrating my life. Although the kids could not see the battle that was being waged in my inner being, Debra recognized it and often asked about it. I didn't realize at the time that it's an insult to tell someone that you hate the fact that you love them, but one day I told Debra how I felt. As she walked into the room where I was sitting, I was wondering how I could suppress the feelings I didn't like.

She asked, "What's up, Fred?"

I said, "Nothing. I'm just tripping, because I don't like how I been feeling."

She turned to me and asked, "What feelings? You still tripping on your condition?"

I said, "No, but I think I'm starting to love you."

She stopped and with a big smile approached me, then she said, "Aww! Fred, I love you, too."

I said, "You don't understand. I hate how I feel because I can't do what I want to."

Her reaction was as if I had just slapped her; the smile went away, and a look of anger mixed with sadness took its place.

Although she said nothing about what I had just told her, the damage had been done. For a woman who already thought she wasn't worth loving, my words stung with the force of a 1,000-volt charge, and she felt every watt. I didn't hide my anger, nor did I make excuses for it, but I now recognize that those few words hurt our relationship more than anything else could have. Even though after that day Debra and I never talked about how I was feeling, I noticed her attitude began to change after our conversation in the room. Debra somehow got it in her head that the reason I didn't want to love her was because I loved Dawn. What she didn't understand was that I had never felt real love for another person. I had been self-centered and selfish for so long I couldn't understand the unselfishness of love. I hated being overwhelmed with the unselfish emotions love evoked in me.

Soon, our house became a war zone that not only affected Debra and me; the kids suffered as well. Many nights we went at it—arguing, yelling, and fighting, which always ended with Debra packing up her and the kids' things to go to her mother's house. I can only imagine what the kids were thinking during those times or how they felt seeing us fight. We were so lost in our feelings that we totally ignored theirs. In one-year period we repeated this scene at least twenty times, sometimes only weeks apart. Our arguing caused the kids to act out and begin to fight amongst each other. Jai and Vonne went at it the worst, because they always drew blood. Either Jai was hitting Vonne, or Anita was beating on them both. There wasn't any peace in our house. The irony was that we truly loved each other, but that love became the source of our problems: instead of bringing us together, it tore us apart.

Two years after the conversation in the room, Debra and I separated for good. I had been up all night spending our last money on drugs while the kids and Debra slept. When they awoke, we were broke, and all I wanted to do was sleep. However, instead of sleep, Debra and I started arguing. Debra asked, "Fred, where's the money that was in my coat?"

I said, "I don't know. You sure you put it there?" We both knew I was lying, and that day was the last straw for Debra.

"Fred, I know where I put my money!" She yelled.

I said, "I took it. The money is gone, so get over it!"

I really thought it would be like all the other times, but I didn't realize that would be the last day Debra and I would share a home.

The holy grail of our family was a picture Debra and I had taken before I was shot. This picture was a reminder of what had once been, and Debra protected it with all her might, but that day while we were arguing in a fit of rage, she grabbed the picture and tore it up, yelling, "You can't give me nothing!"

I was at a loss. Although I had witnessed it, I still could not believe it, nor did I realize that this time was different. That day, Debra and the kids packed up like she had done many times before, and I can still remember being happy that they were leaving so I could go to sleep.

Three days after they left, I became sick and had to go to the hospital. I was in the hospital for two weeks, and on the fourth day Debra came up to the hospital to bring me some weed and to talk. Although she was still mad, she wanted to come home, but after they left I realized I could not go on the way I was going. I decided to start trying to change. As Debra and I sat down in the outside visiting area to roll the weed, she asked, "Fred, do you want me to come home?"

I said, "That's what I wanted to talk to you about." I turned to face her and said, "Debra, listen, I don't want you to come back. I need to learn to take care of myself. I have these two boys, and I don't want them to continue seeing me like this. I want to be able to teach them how to be a man, but I can't if I'm not a man, so give me some time."

She smiled and said, "I understand, Fred. I think that's good."

Love Lost, but Independence Found

What I didn't know was that these were the very words that Debra wanted to hear. While we could not hold our relationship together, we still loved each other. That love was the binding force that has kept our family together over the years. Once I got out of the hospital, Debra came to the house and showed me how to wash clothes, cook the foods I liked, and an easy way for me to clean the house. She was like a proud mother who was helping her child to become independent.

As she was leaving, Debra asked, "You want me to check in on you next week, Fred?"

I responded, "No, Debra. I have to do this on my own."

She nodded. "Fred, I'm so proud of you, but if you need me—call."

As Debra walked out the door that day, I really thought that would be that, but I didn't understand the power of love. In the past I had always been able to just walk away from women, but I guess it was because I never loved them. However, three weeks after our separation, I was lovesick, and all I wanted was my wife. I missed her face, her voice, and especially her smile, but I couldn't bring myself to call or go see her. I suffered in silence. For the first month and a half I stayed in bed—until one hot summer night in 2000 when I just couldn't take it anymore. I got dressed and started for her mother's house, but when I arrived, Debra wasn't there. I left and went into the neighborhood looking for her. I found her on Leavenworth and Eddy Street in the Tenderloin with a bunch of young men and women.

I asked, "Debra, can you come talk to me?" She agreed and I said, "Come home—I miss you."

Debra had been in the streets having fun since she left my house, and she wasn't about to give it up for me. While we were talking, the people she was with were ready to go, and they kept yelling, "Debra, you coming or what?"

I asked her, "Are you going with them or me?"

To my surprise, she said, "Fred, I'm going with them, so go home."

The journey home from the point where I left Debra was about ten blocks, but that night, it felt more like ten miles. Debra's words were not what I wanted to hear or what I expected, so they hurt me to the very core. All the way home, I felt as if my heart were being torn out of my chest, and it got worse with each block. I thought, *"How can I go on without her?"* She had been a constant fixture in my life for nine years. I could only think of the loss. I missed her, but the thought that she would one day come home had kept me going, but that night the dream was shattered.

As I approached the house, the sight of the apartment building was overcast in my mind with gloom, sadness, and loneliness. I felt as if I were a tree that had been uprooted by the raging of the wind; my roots had been exposed, and there would be no way to replant them, so I was to just wither and die, or so I thought.

Three months after Debra and I separated, her younger sister Lita started to come by. Lita was like a breath of fresh air throughout the house. She cleaned, cooked, and catered to my every need; except for sex, she took care of me just as well as Debra. Each morning at about seven o'clock, Lita would be knocking on my door. Once she entered the house, she would instantly tell me to get up and bust my move (meaning shower and get dressed). I reasoned that she did this because she felt uncomfortable being in the house with me half-dressed. About a month after she started to come by, she motivated me to go downstairs and do my walking. Each morning for a year and a half we went downstairs after breakfast, and she helped me walk. I would walk back and forth ten times on the patio or until I couldn't walk any more.

Though most of the young men I used to hang out with were nonexistent in my life, at that time there were some who stayed by my side. Among the men who came to help me were A.J. and Chucky-B. Each in his own time and his own way helped me walk. When A.J. found out that I was relearning how to walk, he was the first to run to my side. He would come by during the times I was walking and support me. Although I had love for A.J. before, his help proved to me that he also had love for me. A.J. didn't like to see me on the walker, so he would tell me to use him. He stood in front of me with his hands out, and I placed mine in his. He then became the source of not only my physical support but my mental support as well. I began to get stronger both mentally and emotionally as I was working to strengthen my legs. Just as A.J. flew to my side once the announcement came that I was walking, Chucky-B soared in to aide me as well.

Chuck often came by the house, but unlike the others, he never wanted to sit and talk. He always got me up and out of the house to do my walking. Chuck was five years younger, but he was the closest member to me in Nine-Deep. While I was walking, Chuck was always with me. He would stop me as I drove through

Third Street so he could get in the car to ride with me as I made my rounds of the city. Chuck stopped by the house at least once a week. The Metreon was a small mall that was a short four blocks away from my house, but on my walker, it was as if it were across the city. Each time Chuck appeared, we would start the journey together. It took me the better part of a year from the day that we started to accomplish the goal that we had set together. Even though my walking was getting better, I still clung to the wheelchair—mainly because I never wanted the women in my life to see me struggling to walk.

My woman at the time was a beautiful young girl named Alexis. Alexis and I met through my nephew, Andrew, and she quickly became my focus. At the time, I was about thirty-one, and Alexis was an immature young lady, but we made it work. I thought it was wrong to mess with a lady of her young years, but my loneliness overrode my common sense. Except for the young men who occasionally stopped by, I was completely alone, so her company was invaluable. I didn't intend to start a relationship with her, but one day out of the blue she called me.

I answered the phone. "Hello."

Alexis said, "Tootie, this Alexis. Can we talk?"

"What's on your mind?"

She said, "I was drinking with a friend and her boyfriend, but I must have passed out because I can't remember how I got on the couch."

I asked, "You all right?"

She responded, "Yeah, but I don't have any clothes on. I think they did something to me."

I told her, "First of all get dressed, and I'll stay on the phone with you until the sun comes up, but when it does, get out of there."

I guess it was the concern I showed for her wellbeing that made her attracted to me, but whatever it was, we became close that night. After that night, Alexis called me almost every night. We talked and laughed, and through our conversations, we developed a connection. Our friendship was platonic, but it was extremely satisfying. I wasn't missing sex—I was missing intimacy. Even though she was young, our friendship became to me like a rose that grew out of the concrete, which was something amazing. Alexis was a curly-haired, caramel-complexioned young lady who stood about 5'7" and had a beautiful personality. On more than one occasion, she would come over and let me cook for her on weekends. After we ate, we would watch TV and talk for hours at a time. Even though she helped my spirit more than words can articulate, her presence was also a great interruption in my walking. While I was home alone, I used the walker to get around, but when she came over I went back to using the wheelchair. Finally, I reasoned out a way that I would be forced to walk, but I must say, it was a ridiculous plan.

After four months of chilling with Alexis and one day after she had gone home, I decided I didn't need the wheelchair anymore. I was fed up with how it hindered my walking, and I knew it would always be a problem as long as it was in the house. One day, I awoke with a plan: I would take the chair to the Oakland airport and leave it there. That was as far as my limited thinking had reasoned, and how I would get home afterwards never really crossed my mind.

On the morning of October 3, 2001, I awoke, got dressed, and started out for the airport. I made it there two hours later and immediately went straight for the complementary wheelchairs that the airport offered to its customers. I transferred from my chair to theirs and started for the exit. Once I made it to the bus stop, the thought hit me: *How* would I *get on the bus?* The answer came quickly: I would crawl and sit in front.

While the bus driver said nothing, once I made it to the Bay Area Mass Transit Station (BART) they would not let me crawl onto the train. Even though today I can see the stupidity in my decision, at that time I was slowly losing my mind, so it seemed a good idea. During those days, due to my losing touch with reality, I was placed on home detention for a case (criminal conviction) I caught a year earlier because I had chosen to follow a young man back into the streets.

Chapter 5

The Return to Ignorance

While I knew better than to go back to the streets, I was slowly tempted to because I looked at the streets through the eyes of two younger men. After Debra and I separated, there were always young men and women roaming in and out of my house. Two of the young men who stayed with me in the house were Ken and Timmy. Ken lived with me first. I met him when I was a child, and after about ten years, he resurfaced in the Tenderloin needing a place to stay. Ken was four years younger than I was and a flamboyant hustler. He stood 5'7", and his muscular frame and caramel complexion were adored by the young girls of the neighborhood. Ken made his money by breaking into houses and selling the goods he stole. While he lived with me, I wanted for nothing because he took care of all my needs.

In the game, every older man always had a younger one doing his bidding while the younger man was learning the rules and how to hustle in the streets. The saying in the hood is "the game is sold, not told." Hence, on the one hand, Ken was supplying my needs, but on the other hand, I was teaching him the rules of the game we lived by, which worked for both of us. He brought food and weed with him every time he came home. Furthermore, if I needed money or to buy my son something, he always provided it. A year after he moved into my house, he went to jail, but not before introducing me to his friend Timmy.

After Ken went to jail at the end of 2003, Timmy moved in and became my youngster. Unlike Ken, Timmy wasn't a hustler, nor did he want to be, but he went the route of drug addict. In the house, Timmy mostly ran for me. He went to the store, brought me things from the kitchen, and helped take care of my son Vonne. He made his own money, and although it wasn't as much as Ken had made when he was out, Timmy was satisfied. It was Timmy's job to do whatever I asked of him to do without question, but it was my job to instruct him. With Ken, I didn't need to teach him how to get money because he was doing it already. However, Timmy needed hands-on teaching, so one day while we were drinking Timmy said, "Fred, let's go outside and get at some girls."

I was drunk and feeling good, so I said, "Come on, let's go, but where you wanna go?"

He said, "Let's go the Nordstrom's mall on Market Street."

As we walked, I said, "Don't get there and freeze up."

"I won't," He responded. "I talk to girls every day, but you on the other hand ain't hollered at a girl in like twenty years."

I said, "It ain't been that long, but it's like riding a bike: once you learn to do it right, you always know how."

We laughed as he said, "Yeah? We'll see."

We entered the mall on the north side and went straight for the elevators, but as we passed a women's clothing store, a beautiful young Filipino woman caught our attention. She was light-skinned and short, with long flowing dark black hair and a smile that lit up the whole store. Timmy looked at me and said, "There you go, Fred. Let's see if you can pull her." (get her phone number).

I said, "What, you scared? She's only a woman."

He smirked. "Then get her number."

I rolled up to the young lady and asked, "How's your day going?"

She said, "Not too good. It's the last three hours of my shift, and I'm bored."

I asked, "What's the name behind the face?"

She smiled. "My name is Jordan, but how you gon' ask my name before giving me yours?"

I smiled back. "My bad. I was just lost in your beauty, so I forgot, but my name is Traivonne."

"That's a nice name," She said.

At this point, I saw she was open, so I went for the big question and asked, "Jordan, I really would like to know the personality behind the name and face, so if it's cool with you I would like to get yo' number."

She smiled and said, "It's cool, but I work a lot so you gon' have to catch me at night. My number is 415 555-2345." Even though our conversation was on point, I really didn't expect for her to give me her number.

I said, "I have to go, but I would really like to continue this conversation tonight if you have time."

She said, "We'll see if you call."

I rolled back to Timmy with a smirk on my face and a sense of accomplishment in my soul. I said, "The next one is on you."

He just smiled. "What did you say to her?"

I said, "Like I said, once you know, you know." Although it was only one number, it gave me something I thought I would never regain—Confidence.

We left the mall and went into the Tenderloin where my confidence turned into a lust for money. I saw many of the old friends I had been ducking still making money. When I was walking, I was a terror, and the block I represented was feared and hated by many in the city. For that, the people of the neighborhood still respected me. Having boosted my confidence, that night I decided to start hustling again.

I had no money or workers, but I knew I could go to my friend Lenny from the Nine Deep, who by this time was a baller (big time drug dealer) in the neighborhood. I met Lenny on the block and immediately asked, "Lenny, can I get a come up?"

He was willing but asked, "How you gon' push it? Because that will tell me how much to give you."

I said, "I have one youngster that I can get to sell it, but I'm also gon' use dope fiend workers, too."

Lenny was happy I was getting back to the business, so he went to his car and came back with an ounce of crack, handed it to me, and said, "Be careful."

I had three young women, one young man, and countless dope fiend workers pushing the dope on the street, but after three months, I was caught. That day was one of my stupidest. I remember I had to pay a bill, and I had the money on me, but I didn't want to spend my profit until I had made some more money. I went to the block alone and tried to make the hundred dollars I needed. Once I made it to the block, a young man named Markie stopped me and said, "Gz, don't sell on the right side of the block. The police are watching in the building."

I said, "Alright, thanks, but could they see on the left side?"

He shook his head. "No, I been selling on that side all morning."

I said, "Good looking, but while I'm out here watch my back."

He said, "Alright."

Since no one was outside, I made the hundred dollars in ten minutes, but I was stuck on the money so I stayed another hour. As I was leaving, I made the mistake of crossing the street. I was so lost in how fast the money was coming in that I totally forgot what Markie had told me. As I was rolling down the street, a tall, skinny black man of about forty approached me and asked, "Do you have something for fifty?"

I thought to myself, "I can't pass this up," so I backed up on a car, reached into my hidden spot on my wheelchair, and pulled out my sack and served him. After the deal was done, we turned and left, but when he got about ten feet away from me, the police started to chase him. I turned to see him in the middle of the street running and thought to myself, "They saw us." Immediately I turned and rolled down the street.

I was so panicked that I didn't reason right. Before me lay two paths: I could roll straight and throw my dope in the crowd of drug addicts where the police would never have found it, or I could turn right at the corner, roll down a big hill, and pass the police station at the bottom of the hill. I chose the latter, and I rolled down the hill. However, I wasn't as fast as I thought I would be, and at the bottom of the hill stood two police officers awaiting to arrest me. Once I stopped, the two officers grabbed my hands and took me into custody. One said to the other, "Look at all the crack crumbs on his lap."

The other officer tried to pick up the crumbs, saying, "We can package these to send to the lab."

But before he could gather them up, I quickly swept the crumbs off my lap as they watched. After I brushed away the crumbs, the white officer punched me in the chest and said, "You think you slick, huh."

They brought me into the station and placed me in a room by myself to await search. One by one, each officer took turns coming into the room to check me, but none could find my hidden spot. They took off my shoes and socks, and they searched the pockets on my pants, coat, and wheelchair but came up empty. At the same time, the man I was caught with was in another room yelling, "Did y'all catch the man in the wheelchair? It was him that sold it to me and I'll testify to it!"

I just laughed and thought to myself, "*A snitch is just like a woman. Their true nature will come out once they're under pressure.*" By this time, the officers had

given up trying to find the dope, but just as I started to
think I was in the clear, the police officer who saw me
make the sale came in. He went right to my secret spot
and found the dope. All the police officers who knew I
was selling but could not prove it came in and laughed
and threatened me with going to the penitentiary.
However, I wasn't worried: I knew it was my first time
in a long while, so all the court could do was give me
probation—but I still went to jail that night.

I stayed in jail for one week and went to court,
but I was prepared. For three days during that week I
spent in jail, my probation officer Herold Jenkins came
to the jail to see me and help me get ready. Jenkins was a
tall, average-shaped, dark-skinned black man in his late
forties who had a warm and helpful spirit. Jenkins
always tried to keep young black men out of the
penitentiary, but we kept doing things that would land us
there. He came to me after he had gotten off work and
instructed me on what to say and what documents to
bring to court, and he assured me that if I did everything
he said, he would recommend to the court to send me
home.

First, I needed letters witnessing to my character.
I also needed medical documents, and lastly, I needed
either a letter stating I had a job to come home to or a
letter stating I was doing volunteer work with youths.
Although I was in the streets, I knew the value of having

a square woman for times such as these, and Dawn was just that.

I instructed Dawn on what I needed and how to go about getting it, and she went right to work. She had papers with the letterhead from the group home she worked for, so she used them to write a letter stating I was mentoring the children and teaching them about the dangers of the street life. Then she had her mother who was a legal secretary for a respected San Francisco attorney write a letter stating I was volunteering at her office and learning the law. Also, there were letters from Dawn's coworkers commending my turnaround and praising my character. Dawn had also gotten together all my medical records, both mental and physical, and lastly she wrote a letter stating we had just had a baby, and she needed me around the house to help out with his care. Along with these letters and documents, I also had an outstanding probation report and Mr. Jenkins' recommendation. Just as Mr. Jenkins had told me, two days later the judge had no problem sending me home on my own recognizance, and he set my trial for two months away.

The trial was held at the hall of justice in San Francisco in a small court room on the third floor of the building. As I rolled into the court room, there were three lawyers standing to my left talking; however, I could not see my lawyer. Two people sat in the gallery staring at the lawyers, trying to hear what they were saying. After about ten minutes, a short, middle aged white woman entered the courtroom carrying a hand full of files, which she sat on the table to my left. Two minutes after that, the judge appeared out of a back room as a bailiff yelled, "All rise!"

The trial began like all the other trials I had been in, but there was one thing that was different, and that was me. While awaiting trial and at home, I had a spiritual awakening, so once the trial started, I had already made up mind that I wouldn't lie.

As my trial began, I leaned over to my lawyer and asked, "Is the plea offer still on the table?"

Before going to trial, the district attorney had offered a deal: If I pled guilty to "sale of a controlled substance," I would receive three years' probation and three months home detention. I didn't take the deal because my lawyer assured me they would come with a better deal at the trial. However, I knew I was guilty and needed to be punished. In light of my spiritual awakening and the fact that I didn't want to lie, I decided to take the deal. My lawyer stood up and asked to approach the bench.

Both lawyers rose and started for the bench, and after a few minutes they went back to their places while the judge spoke to the court. He said, "We have a plea agreement between the district attorney and the plaintiff." Then he turned to me and asked, "Mr. Howard, do you understand your rights?

I responded, "Yes."

"Do you understand that by taking this plea you give up your right to not self-incriminate yourself and your right to a speedy trial?"

I said, "Yes."

The judge then addressed the court and said, "I accept the plea agreement and enter it into the record." He turned back to me and said, "Mr. Howard, it is alleged that on the day of the 18th in the month of March in the year of 2003, you engaged in the act of selling a controlled substance. Please explain in your own words what happened on that day."

As everyone turned and looked at me, I said, "I was rolling down the street of Ellis in the Tenderloin when a man asked me if I had something for fifty and I said yes. I then backed up on a car, reached behind me into my stash spot on my wheelchair, grabbed a small bag of crack, pulled out fifty dollars' worth, and gave it to him."

The court was shocked because I told it as the police report had reported it. I left nothing out, nor did I try to make excuses, but I threw myself on the mercy of the judge.

He said, "I don't think that I have ever had anyone tell it as plainly as you did today. For your honesty, I will amend the agreement to only two months' home detention. However, if you don't complete the sentence I'll retrial you on the case, and you may end up going to the penitentiary."

I said, "Thank you—I'll complete it."

While on home detention in the winter of 2004, I had another spiritual awakening. Although I was not a religious man, nor did I attend church as a child, my eyes suddenly turned to the Bible. In those days, there were always young girls who moved in and out of my house; one such girl was Reanna. Reanna was a twenty-year-old dark-skinned African American woman. She stood a towering 5'11", and her frame was a thick 170 lbs. Reanna and I met when she was twelve in the Tenderloin area of San Francisco. Now that she was a grown woman, we spent most of our days sitting around the house smoking weed and snorting cocaine. One night, we were up partying until the early morning. I went to bed that night high, and I had always hated anything that seemed religious, but when I woke up, all I wanted was a Bible. I dug out an old Bible I had hidden a long time ago under my clothes in the bottom of one of my dresser drawers.

Before I could read, I felt I had to clean my house. So, I got a bucket, filled it with soap and water, and started to wipe down my walls. I sat on my butt on the floor and I started on the right side of the front door and moved slowly around the house until I arrived at the other side of the door. Once that was done, I mopped and swept the floors. What was amazing was to sweep the floors I had to move two couches, an entertainment center, and a king-sized bed in my wheelchair! After cleaning the house from top to bottom, I sat down on the loveseat and started to read. As I read, my life flashed before my mind, and I prayed for forgiveness for the pain I had caused others.

Forgiveness is given when there is repentance, and even though I didn't yet understand repentance, I was actively repenting. As situations passed before my mind, I would weep, mourn, and ask for the person's forgiveness. The way in which I treated the women in my life came to mind, and I begged each one to forgive me for my actions. Then there was the pain I caused men, which brought me to my knees. I was forced to realize that I was a walking, talking source of pain to all who came in my direction, and it hurt. I repeated this scene each night for three weeks, and after it had passed I felt like a new man. Although my spirit had been cleansed, my mind was now to be tested, and the test would lead to insanity. Due to the separation with my wife, the loss of my kids, the drugs, and my inability to walk, I fell into a deep depression and slowly lost touch with reality.

The Battle with Insanity

I never questioned my sanity during those days, but those around me could see that I was slowly going mad. In the summer of 2005, my nephew Andrew came to live with me. He was giving my sister trouble, so she thought he needed a man's touch. Andrew was a light-skinned young man who stood about 6'0" and was searching for his identity. What he was looking for he saw in my past, and so he loved and idolized me.

Andrew was the first to recognize that my mind was slipping. He would later tell me that many times I would sit in the living room staring into space or talking and laughing to myself. Due to my loneliness and drug habit, my mind had created a different personality to keep me entertained. I remember that voice in my head was like a good friend. It was there when I arose and when I lay down. I would ask it questions and it would give me the answers, but I never questioned if the answers were true. It would give me visions that were funny but at other times frightening. It all came to a head one day, and I completely lost it.

During those times, I spent more time in mental institutions than I did at home. There were times when I was dirty and sitting on the same blocks where I sold drugs and robbed people. One day I awoke sitting on Market Street in San Francisco with no shoes, no wheelchair, or walker. As I sat there, a young man I once wanted to rob and didn't care too much for walked up on me as I was talking to myself. He asked, "Fred, what's up?"

I was in a reality of my own fashioning, so I neither saw him nor responded back, but he kept trying. As he stood there, he began to roll up a blunt, (weed in a cigar paper), and even though I had looked past him, I saw that blunt. So I asked, "Tommy, can I hit it?"

He said, "Yeah, just let me roll it."

As he rolled the blunt, he called my ex-girlfriend Tunisia, who just so happened to be in the city that day. Even though Tunisia and I had not been in a relationship for many years, we were still the best of friends. She immediately drove to where I was to see if she could help. Tommy stayed with me the whole time to make sure I didn't leave or hurt myself before Tunisia arrived. As I saw that Tommy had finished rolling the blunt, I asked, "Tommy, when you light it up are you gon' let me hit it?"

Although he kept saying I could hit it, he never passed it to me. I later learned that Tunisia had told him not to pass it to me.

As Tunisia drove up, I looked at Tommy and said, "Pass it to me before Tunisia get out."

Tommy's response was, "Sure you can hit it."

Tunisia jumped out of the car and could not believe what she saw. Her first words were, "Stop playing, Fred. Get up."

Looking past her and staring into the distance, I said, "Tunisia, what you doing here?"

With tears in her eyes and a look filled with compassion, she broke down. Not knowing what to do to help me, she called my older sister Shawn and told her of my condition and location. As she was on the phone, a police car drove up and asked if everything was all right. Shawn told Tunisia to call the hospital and have me admitted, so she walked up to the police car and asked if they could call the mental health department because I needed to go the psychiatric hospital. That day was the scariest experience of that time, because I could have done anything, and anything could have been done to me. When the ambulance pulled up, the technicians jumped out and rushed to me.

As they walked up, they asked, "Has he taken any drugs?"

The young man who had been with me barked back at them in an angry tone, "He don't do drugs!"

Out of all the people I knew in that neighborhood, it's funny that the only one who thought enough of me to help was someone I didn't like. That young man showed me that *I should be careful of the*

*people I alienate because they just might be the ones to
save my life.* None of the people I once called friends
took the time to see if I was all right, but many of them
saw me. Talking to some of them after I came out of the
fog, I found that the reason that most gave as to why they
didn't help was that they didn't know what to do to help.
However, I neither believed nor accepted that excuse
because neither did Tommy, but he at least tried. For the
next three years, I would go through scenes like this one
over and over again in cities like Oakland, Concord, and
Sacramento.

The first time I took my insanity on the road was
in December of 2005, when I traveled to Oakland,
California. During those days, the voices in my head
were all I could focus on, and even though Andrew
stayed with me, we hardly ever talked. Many nights
Andrew would come home and want to talk, but all I
could do was stare at him (or past him), so he started
staying out late—which gave the voices in my head the
time they needed to take complete control over my
thoughts. One night, I was fed the thought that if I made
it to an apartment in Oakland, my big brother Richie
would show up to give me power. The only catch was I
had to make it there without talking to anyone. At the
time, I lived on 6th and Howard Street in San Francisco,
and the Greyhound bus station was a short ten blocks
away, so I tried to make the journey. I never did make it
there silently because although my mouth stayed closed

my mind was always active, so I kept talking to myself in my head. I tried at least twenty times before I made it to Oakland.

On my final trip to the Greyhound station, I realized that if I sang in my head, it kept the voices from speaking. Therefore, this is what I did. I started out early because I was now on a walker, which slowed me down a great deal. As I walked, I sang an old song my mom had taught me as a child in my head. With each step, I was more convinced that at the end of the journey, I would be on my way to heaven.

Although I was in a fog, many of the old drug addicts I used to sell to kept asking for drugs, which made it hard for me not to speak. One man named Billy followed me a block and a half, asking for a ten-shot the whole way. I just kept my head down and mentally sang, "Jesus loves me this I know because the Bible tells me so."

I made it to the Greyhound station an hour later. Although I had no money and no ticket, I was convinced that I would make it to Oakland. I stood in line for twenty minutes, and when the door to board the bus opened, I walked through like everyone else. I climbed up the stairs of the bus and sat down in a seat.

The bus driver started to ask to see tickets, but I paid him no attention. As he walked up to me he said, "Excuse me, sir: can I see your ticket?"

I looked at him and turned my head. He asked, "Would you like to buy a ticket?"

My response was, "I'm going to Oakland to get my power." He just gave me a sympathetic look and moved on.

Once in Oakland, an address popped into my head. I thought it would be there that I would meet Richie, so I decided to go. I had not been in Oakland in years, and I didn't know my way around, so I went directly for the taxi cabs and jumped into one. The man behind the wheel was a chubby, caramel-complexioned Arab man who looked like he was in his late fifties. He helped me into the cab and then asked, "Where we going tonight?"

I gave him the address, and without another word, he turned around and sped off.

We arrived at the address in fifteen minutes and the man said, "That will be eight dollars and thirty-five cents." I looked at him as if he had said something in Russian and started to get out the cab. He tried to lock the doors, but I had already opened the left back door and was halfway out. He asked, "Hey, you gon' pay me or what?"

I said, "Wait here. I'm going to get my power and then I'll pay you."

"You blacks think you don't have to pay for anything, just get out!" He barked at me.

I stood in front of the building looking for a way in, and just as I started for the door, a man came out, which gave me my way in.

Once in the building a number came to my mind, which I believed was the apartment I needed to go to, so I started for the elevator. I really didn't see the danger in what I was about to do, nor did I understand that this reality I was living in was one of my own making. I hurried to the door of apartment 23 and knocked.

An old woman asked, "Who is it?"

I responded, "It's me."

She said, "How can I help you?"

I said, "I need to come into your house, sit on your couch, and wait on my big brother Richie, because he gon' bring my power."

There was a long pause of dead silence, but then the woman opened the door and said, "You ain't coming in here, so get out of here. If you don't leave, I'll call the police." She then quickly closed the door in my face.

I had already come all the way to Oakland with the thought of gaining power; now, I was right at the door to get it, and I was being denied. A sudden sadness took hold of me, and in a desperate plea for entrance, I banged on the door, begged, and cried, but the woman was unmoved. I stood at that door crying until the police showed up. One officer was black, and the other was white. Once they arrived, the woman emerged from the door and explained what had transpired.

They then turned to me and asked, "Do you know anyone who lives in this building?"

I said, "No, but I need to be here to get my power from my brother."

They looked at each other, and the other officer asked, "What power?"

I responded, "The power to go to heaven."

"Where do you live?"

"I live in San Francisco."

"Is there anyone you would like us to call for you so you can get home?" The officer asked.

I barked back, "I can't leave—Richie gon' bring my power, so I have to be here!"

They didn't know what to do with me at this point. I had answered every question they asked accurately, but they could see that there was something not right about me. They could not just let me walk off or stay there, but they didn't know what to do with me either. The black officer asked the other officer to call the supervisor to get instructions on what to do. I watched as he walked off with his hand on the button of the radio. I could not hear what he said to the supervisor, but once he was done talking he said, "We need to get him to John George."

I didn't know who or what John George was (the Alameda County psychiatric hospital), so I agreed to go, but once there I knew I had made a mistake. There was no way out. As we pulled up to the door of John George, I tried to ask the officers if I could just go home, but one answered, "We here now. It's too late for that."

However, he assured me that it was a nice place and went so far as to say people beg to go to this place. I felt better about going in after his words—until I saw the inside.

I admit that my mind was unclear all the way to Oakland and that the reality I had chosen to believe was a delusion, but once in that place, I quickly snapped out of it. As I walked in, I saw men and women sitting and standing around, some scratching, some staring into the distance, and some yelling at the top of their lungs. One man kept yelling, "I am Satan!" and "I will kill everyone in here!"

The people who worked there sat behind a desk and acted as if nothing was wrong, but I saw that nothing was right. The staff didn't help or answer questions. They would only say, "You have to ask the therapist." I never felt so out of place in my life because there was no one to talk to or who could help me.

John George was like stepping into a different world where everyone was insane. Even the counselors acted as if they were out of their minds. They stood behind a desk and oversaw the patients, but they were unsympathetic to their conditions. Each person there contributed to the overall atmosphere in their own way. I was left to my own delusions and the voices in my head.

I sat there for about two hours, and then a young lady came to me and asked, "Are you hungry?"

I asked, "When can I go home?"

"Where is home?" She asked.

I said, "I live in San Francisco."

She responded, "You have to speak to the therapist. If they think you are okay to go home, then they will call your family to come pick you up."

"When will that be?"

"The therapists will be here in the morning, but until then, there is nothing that can be done, so you are going to have to wait."

By the time the therapist arrived for work, I was completely lucid, and all I wanted to do was go home. It took them until lunchtime to get around to seeing me. When they did, they asked me, "What is your name? Do you know what city you are in, and why did you come all the way to Oakland last night?"

I knew if I told the truth, they would not let me go home, so I lied. "My name is Frederick, and I'm in Oakland. The reason that I came to Oakland last night was to see a friend. However, once I made it to Oakland I got confused on the address, and that's why I was at that woman's door last night."

That explanation was all that they needed to hear.

The therapist said, "I think you are all right to go home, but you have to wait until I finish your paperwork, and then we will call your family to come get you."

I thought, "*Home, finally.*" Home seemed to me a distant memory but a welcome one.

With the confirmation that I was going home, a new problem arose—who would come get me? No one in my family but Richie drove, and no one could ever catch up with him. I was stuck in that place. As I was thinking about how to get out, I looked around to see a man standing in the middle of the floor with his pants around his ankles, a woman sitting Indian-style and pulling at her hair laughing uncontrollably, and the staff acting as if none of this was happening and this were just another day at work. I shuddered at the thought of staying there.

Once I was okayed to call for my pickup, I called
Shawn, because she was in Oakland. She said, "Tootie,
I'm gon' ask my girlfriend but don't count on it." I tried
Richie next, not because I thought he would answer but I
just wanted to leave him a message. Richie and I had
always been close, and I reasoned that if he knew where
I was then he would drop everything and come to my
rescue. To my surprise, he answered but he told me,
"Tootie, I don't have my car—I crashed it two nights
ago."

At that, I felt hopeless and struggled with the
thought that I might not be going home after all. When
the therapist came in and asked how long would it take
for my ride to come, she must have seen it on my face
because she just said, "Let me see what I can do." An
hour later she reappeared and said, "We called an
ambulance to come pick you up, and they will be here in
an hour." I will never forget the elation that swept over
me. It was like the shining of the sun after a rainy day,
which brought with it a beautiful vibrantly colored
rainbow. An hour later, I was on my way home, but due
to my complete break with reality I had totally forgotten
I was on home detention.

Chapter 6

The Turning Point

My mental breakdown and the subsequent AWOL placed me in a peculiar situation, which terrified me on the ride home. I walked out of the court one day relieved and assured that I wouldn't go back, but I found out no man knows the future. The penitentiary was a good motivator for me to finish the program, plus I loved my freedom and shuddered to think of losing it. But now that I had left the house and been gone for three days, my freedom, my home, and my income were all in jeopardy. I had a bigger problem to deal with, because my mental state was far from stable.

Once I made it home, I went straight to the shower and then to bed, but the voices in my head kept me up with thoughts of "the pen." I knew that it would take at least four weeks for the record of my whereabouts to be transferred to the court and for them to put out a warrant, so I tried to stay around the house and not open the door for people who knocked. During those days, I hated the night, especially the times between midnight and 6:00 AM, because it was during those times that my anxiety was at its highest.

I imagined myself in the court standing before the judge, hearing him say, "I sentence you to three years in the state penitentiary." In my ignorance, I could not wait to go to the pen, but now, after experiencing life, love, and family, I feared losing the relationships I had built. Although I knew I was looking at jail time, I kept going outside, and many nights I slept with the door unlocked. The thoughts and the voices that caused them were full of activity and progression like the inside of a beehive; the result was the destruction of my sanity.

By this time, Andrew had gone back home to his mom's house and I was left to my thoughts and the voices in my mind, which left me easy prey for the police. A month after my excursion, the police came looking for me. One day as I approached my apartment building, I saw three officers going into the building, so I hid in the store on the corner and waited to see what would happen. They stayed in the building for about twenty minutes, then they came out and jumped into their patrol car and left. Even with this close call, I still didn't protect myself or keep my door locked. It was only a matter of time before I would get caught, but I was so in my mind that I never thought about going to jail. Thought and action are completely separate, so even though I didn't think of jail, I still ended up there five days later. After I saw the police in my building, I still didn't get it.

I had gotten into the habit of not answering the door when people knocked or called from downstairs, so as the officers knocked, I just laid there. The officers stood outside the door for two minutes, and then I heard one of them ask the others, "Hey, did y'all check the door?"

When I heard that, I instantly looked at the door, and from where I was on the bed, I could see that I hadn't locked it the night before. I just put the blanket over my head and hoped that they didn't turn the knob. My hopes were dashed as a tall muscular white man stood over my bed and asked the question no man with a warrant wants to hear.

He said, "Are you Frederick Howard?"

I looked up, acted as if I didn't hear him, and said, "Huh, what you say?"

He asked again, "Are you Frederick Howard?"

I was caught. "Yeah, why?"

He didn't respond to my question: he just grabbed my arm. "Get up—you're under arrest."

"Can I take my walker and braces?" I asked.

"Yeah, but hurry up and get dressed."

They took me to the San Francisco County jail, processed me, gave me a bedroll, and stuck me in the hospital ward. I thought that was good thing because I would not have to get up early like the rest of the inmates. I didn't realize that I would come to hate that privilege. Indeed, for three weeks it was beautiful, but every day after that, it was as if I were chained to the

130

bed. There were two other inmates in the room with me, which made watching TV a battle. Each of us liked certain TV programs, and none of us liked the others' programs, so we argued constantly. Even though we were all disabled, we still had our bad attitudes and a lot of aggression. In the far right bed was a young man who had a withered arm. His name was Conrad, a 5'5", dark-skinned black man who for some reason didn't like me. In the middle bed was Trey; he was cool and didn't bother anyone, unless it was about the TV. He was 6'2", very light-skinned, had only one leg, so he didn't really get out of bed that much. One day, Conrad and I started to argue over the TV.

As I turned the TV on, I looked over at the other beds and noticed that the men appeared to be sleeping, so I turned to *CSI New York*. *CSI* was a cop drama where at the end of the program the bad guy always was caught and sent to jail, so Conrad hated it. As soon as the theme song began to play, Conrad looked up and asked me, "Why you changed it? I was watching that program."

I said, "Man, you were sleep. If you were watching it, what happened before the commercial came on?"

He couldn't answer me but said, "Man, I'm not trying to hear all that, but all I know if you don't turn it back I'm coming over there."

I called his bluff. "If you come anywhere near me I'm gon' beat you with that walker, and if you think I'm playing then try me."

He said, "Whatever!" But he never got up or tried me for the rest of my stay in the dorm.

Although lying in bed was bad, not being able to speak to my son Vonne was much worse. For the first three weeks, I tried to think of someone who would accept my collect calls, but everyone I tried denied me. I didn't communicate with Vonne the whole time, so I was a mess. I missed him and our daddy-and-son talks, but halfway through the fourth week, I thought of Alexis and called her. I knew Alexis liked me, but what I didn't understand was that she actually loved me. Even though I had broken up with her, she still had my back.

After she answered the phone, I said, "What's up, baby?"

She quickly answered, "Baby? I thought you didn't want to be with me, so now I'm your baby?"

I said, "Come on, don't do that. You know I care about you, but you're too young for me. I told you. I just can't mess with anyone younger than my little sister. If I knew an older man was messing with her I would be ready to hurt someone, so I won't do it. But I need to ask a favor of you."

She said, "What is it, Fred? I'm not coming up there to see you or putting money on your books. So what is it you want?"

"I don't need anything like that, but I do need you to call my son for me."

"Oh, I guess I can do that as long as it's only a call or two a day, because my mom pays the bill." She said.

"All right I won't burn you out, but here's the number."

As she clicked over to make the call, an officer was yelling in the dorm that we had twenty minutes until lights out.

The next thing I heard was Vonne's voice saying, "Hello? Is this you, Dad?"

"Yeah, Vonne," I responded. "It's me. How you been doing, and have you been listening to your mom?"

He said, "Yeah, but I miss going to your house, Dad. When can I come over?"

I told him, "Vonne, you can't come this week, but maybe next week."

This was my answer to that question each week, because Vonne always asked to come over each time we talked. Then one night as we were talking, Vonne asked me a different question.

He asked, "Dad, do you still love me?"

I was shocked. "Vonne, why did you ask that? Of course I love you."

He said, "It's because you don't want me to come over your house. If you loved me you would want to see me—right, Dad?"

I have never been so shocked or hurt in my entire life. I broke down. "Vonne, me not letting you come to my house doesn't have anything to do with if I love you or not. You can't come because I'm not home. Your dad did something stupid, and I have to pay for it. I'm in jail, Vonne, but as soon as I get out I'm coming to get you, so don't worry."

He said, "All right, Dad. I love you always," and then he hung up.

After we hung up, I realized something that had escaped me all his life: someone cares if I'm not around; someone lives on me and if I die or am trapped, then so is he. That moment changed my whole way of thinking about life. I promised myself that day that I would not come back to jail ever again. I asked myself why I kept getting caught, and a simple answer came back: it wasn't that the police were smart, but it was because I kept doing stupid stuff that landed me in jail. I decided right then that when I got out that I wouldn't do anything that could cause me to come back to jail.

Even though on one hand I was making good
decisions, on the other hand I was still losing my mind.
Day by day, I slowly slipped away from the reality that
surrounded me and into the world within my mind,
which was dominated by the voices inside my head. In
the beginning, I loved to listen and ask questions of the
voices, but that soon came to an end. The voices changed
from helpers to tormentors, and I was stuck in that reality
with them. I no longer had the ability to live in both
worlds. I was trapped in the world of my mind, and it
was a hostile place. Each voice held within it the power
to frighten or encourage, but there were more voices that
chose to torment than there were those that helped. I was
constantly in a state of panic, which manifested in me
constantly talking to myself. Before, I had the power to
ask questions, but all at once I lost that ability as the
voices began to talk though my mouth. To the outside
world, I was crazy and just talking nonsense, but I
understood each word and what it was related to. From
the outside it appeared I held no power over my actions
or my mouth, but inside I was as sane as the next person.

By the fall of 2006, everyone around me had
written me off as insane. No one bothered to hide their
true feelings about me and my situation. They thought I
couldn't understand them, but I understood every look,
word, and motive. It was like I was trapped inside my
mind, and all I could do was watch and listen. Many
times, I witnessed my closest friends laugh or try to

avoid me. I saw family members connive to steal my money and watched as the kids made fun of me for constantly talking to myself. I was rejected by my sisters and left in a house with no food or furniture while I was on a walker with a hurt knee and deemed half-crazy by my big brother. I became an outcast and was passed around from house to house, and all the while I knew that I really wasn't wanted. My insanity and the disposition of my family towards me lasted for three years, and then slowly the Lord brought me out.

The Battle Back to Sanity

After being kicked out of my big sister Shawn's house for the third time, I called my ex-girlfriend Tunisia and said, "Tunisia, can you come get me? Shawn is kicking me out again."

She said, "Why, Tootie, what you do?"

I answered, "Nothing, I just asked her for my money she was holding for me. She said 'You didn't give me no money,' but I know I did, so we got into an argument and she said, 'Get out.'"

Tunisia said, "I'll be there in thirty minutes."

"I'll be outside waiting. She wants me out now."

As I stood in the parking lot of Shawn's apartment building, I wondered where to go, but little did

I know Tunisia had already prepared me a place to go. Tunisia lived in Oakland at the time, which was a short twenty-minute drive to Concord where Shawn was living. The whole time I was waiting, I was stressing about where I would lay my head that night.

Tunisia showed up twenty-five minutes after we talked on the phone and said, "Tootie, you can stay at my house until you find somewhere to go."

I was relieved. "Thanks."

She then asked, "Tootie, what happened?"

I said, "I was saving my money so I could get an apartment. I had saved close to thirteen hundred dollars, but I would spend some on cigarettes and soda. Shawn saw me doing this, so she said to me, 'Give me yo' money, Tootie, so you don't spend it all up,' and I did, but when I asked her for it, she said, 'You didn't give me no money.' She thought I didn't remember because I was crazy, but I knew everything I did no matter what I looked like or acted like at the time. I wouldn't let it go, and eventually we began to argue, and she told me to get out."

"That's scan'less (scandalous)," Tunisia said.

"You telling me."

On the drive to Oakland, Tunisia and I talked about friends we used to hang out with and laughed about situations we often found ourselves in while hustling. She asked if I had my meds, and I said yeah. She then asked, "Tootie, have you seen Hen or Jay-Jay?"

I said, "No, but I heard they moved to Sacramento. Why you ask?"

She said, "I don't know; just was wondering, because y'all was so close I just thought y'all would keep up wit' each other."

"I think Hen is mad at me because I had a baby by Dawn."

She shook her head. "You so silly, why did you do that anyways?"

"She wasn't supposed to get pregnant."

"Did you use a condom?"

"No, but I pulled out."

"Nigga, stop lying! If you had, you wouldn't have a baby."

I just gave her my smile that I used when I was caught, and she smiled back and said, "Trying to run that weak shit by me."

Although I had many male friends that I was close to, none were as close as me and Tunisia. The time we spent in that Taco Bell and getting to know each other over the years was instrumental in us staying together even after we separated. She was my conscience, mom, and friend all rolled into one. The thing with Tunisia was that she was hardly ever on my side when I told her a problem; she kept me honest and always helped me to see my part in the problem, which I believe is what a good friend is supposed to do. She was there as I rode the wave of my highs in life, and she was there when that same wave crashed down upon me as I sank beneath its currents in my lows in life. The sensual, passionate love we shared in our relationship had transformed into a love based on principle, devotion, and trust, which is something that is seldom found apart from years of marriage. As we pulled up to her apartment, she started to read me the riot act on what I could and couldn't do in her house—including no smoking.

She told me, "Tootie, I'm hardly ever home, so I won't be any help around the house; but Tootie, the fridge will always be full and the cable will always be on, but please take care of my house."

As she helped me out of the car and into the house, I thanked her and asked, "Where do I sleep?"

Tunisia pointed to a spot in front of the couch. "You could camp out right there, and I'll bring you some pillows and blankets."

Looking around her house, I saw that the walls were a pale white color with spots here and there that were just a little darker than the rest of the walls. Her couch was a brownish leather sectional with one of the cushions missing. The thing that caught my attention was her TV because it was about 50" and covered most of the wall it hung on. After a minute or two, Tunisia appeared out of the back room carrying a pillow and two big comforters.

She threw them on my lap. "Here, make yourself at home, Tootie, because you're welcome here for as long as you need to be here."

I said, "Thank you, Tunisia. You know I love you, right?"

She said, "Yeah, Tootie, I know. I kinda have that effect on men I've been with," as she smiled and walked off.

True to her word, Tunisia was only at the house one or two days out of the week. Some weeks she didn't even show up, so I had free range to do as I pleased. However, I used my freedom to do everything she told me not to do. I smoked in the house, left dishes in the living room, and constantly left her door unlocked as I searched the streets to buy weed. As long as I had my meds, I was sane, but a month after moving in, I ran out of my pills. Because these meds take a few days to wear off after you stop using them, and because by that time Tunisia was only coming once a week, she didn't know that I was off my meds until it was too late.

After the meds wore off, I was out of it, and I didn't understand things, nor did I have the power to stop my actions. If it came to my mind, I did it, and because of that I found myself smoking while Tunisia and her baby were in the house. I'll never forget the last night I spent at her house because for the first time in our relationship, I saw that she had become afraid of me. Early one Sunday morning, Tunisia and her daughter came in the house. The first thing they both said was, "Dang, Tootie, it stank in here. Move over so I could open the window." I had no power over my actions then, so it was hard to remember to go to the bathroom—so I wore men's briefs. Since I was by myself most of the time, the brief was dirty, which caused a terrible stench that spread around the house. After Tunisia opened the window, she started for her room, her daughter following. At about eight o'clock at night, Tunisia recognized that there was something wrong, and she started to question me about my meds.

She asked, "Tootie, did you take your meds today?"

I tried to respond truthfully, but all that came out was, "Yeah."

She wasn't taking my word for it so she asked, "Tootie, where are the pills you need for your mind?"

I pointed to the top of the TV. "They up there." But they weren't—I hadn't taken a pill in three weeks, and it was showing.

Tunisia started to search through the pill bottles to find the ones that kept me sane, but she soon found out what I already knew—I was out. She turned to me with a pill bottle in her hand and asked, "Tootie, is this the bottle?"

I said, "Yeah, I think that's the one."

"Why you didn't tell me you were running out of pills?"

"I don't know. I feel fine, so I don't think I need them."

A day later I was talking to myself, smoking in the house, and ignoring her and the baby.

That was the last day I spent in her house. As I sat in the kitchen in front of the stove smoking a cigarette, Tunisia came in and asked, "Tootie, what the hell are you doing? My daughter is in the other room!"

I looked her straight in the eye and said, "I'm smoking," and then I rolled off.

She was shocked and came in the living room behind me, but I was out of it, and she knew it, so she called 911. Before the ambulance showed up, I was totally out of reality and could not answer Tunisia's simple questions, but when the ambulance technicians came, I instantly became lucid. They asked me, "What's your name? Do you know what city you're in? Could you tell me who the president is?"

To Tunisia's surprise I stated, "My name is Frederick Robert Howard Jr. We are in Oakland, California, and the president is Bush Jr."

They kept questioning me, asking things like, "How do you feel? Would you like to go to the hospital? Are you hearing voices? If so, what are they saying? Do you want to hurt yourself?"

Even though at the time the hospital would have been best, I kept saying, "I'm fine. I don't need to go to the hospital, and no I'm not hearing voices."

The technicians turned to Tunisia and said, "Ma'am, there's nothing we can do. He does not want to hurt himself, and he has answered every one of our questions correctly."

Tunisia turned and looked at me, and with a desperate plea said, "There's something wrong with him. He's not right! There has to be something you can do." In that moment, I saw fear in her eyes, and it hurt me even as I was mentally breaking down. I had never given her any reason to fear me in all the years we had been together, but that day, she was scared to be in the same house with me.

I turned to the technician and said, "It's okay, I'll go with y'all." As the ambulance pulled off, I cried silently to myself because I thought she would never want to see me again.

We arrived at the hospital in no time, and as we entered, the nurse asked, "Is this the patient for John George?"

The tech yelled back at her, "Yeah, he's hearing voices!"

I stayed in the emergency department for about six hours before they took me to John George. The whole time I was there, I was never asked if I had to use the bathroom or if I was hungry. The nurses and doctors completely ignored me. Each time I would try to ask to be taken to the restroom, they would say, "In a minute" or "I'll get the volunteer to take you", but no one ever came. So, when they told me that the ambulance would be picking me up in ten minutes, I was ready to go. As the ambulance pulled up, the nurse came to my bed and asked me one last time if I wanted to hurt myself—I just looked at her. The whole time I was thinking, "If I had wanted to do myself some harm, y'all would have been too late. I sat here for six hours, and no one even came by to check if I wanted a cup of water or if I had chewed my tongue off, but now you care." I was still hearing voices as I entered John George, and they were telling me that all the people there were going to kill me inside that place.

The fear and anxiety I felt because of their words overwhelmed me, and I broke down just when the nurse came and told me to move from the gurney to a wheelchair. As I started to ask for a bed, the ambulance tech just picked me up and sat me in the chair. The atmosphere of the ward was terrifying for me. The walls were a rust color and, coupled with the dim lighting, they produced a room of darkness. There were painted pictures of what appeared to me as demons who never stopped looking at me. It was as if everyone knew something that I didn't. The nurses and intake personnel just let me sit by myself in a corner of the room. Looking around, I saw what insanity really did to people and shuddered, thinking, *"This is how I must look to others."*

The one person that my condition hurt the most was the one I had promised I would never hurt, my son Traivonne. He was a seven-year-old child who didn't understand why his dad couldn't hug or talk to him. I remember one night when we were living with Shawn, that hurt me, but I was powerless to change. As Vonne and Shawn's boys played inside the house, I went to sit on the porch. I must have been out there for almost five hours just looking up at the stars when all of a sudden Vonne appeared out of the door and asked, "Dad, can you come and lie down with me?"

I said, "Yeah, I'll be in there in a minute." After about an hour, he came back to the door and asked again, but I couldn't move.

He just looked at me and asked, "Dad, I'm tired, why you haven't come in yet?"

I just sat there looking up at the stars, but my heart hurt more that night than any other during that period in my life. I thought to myself as I looked into his eyes, "All he wants is me, and I can't even hug him and tell him everything will be all right." I was under the power of the voices in my mind, and they had no compassion for his pain or pleas. He turned around and went to bed without me. Once he left, my emotions were all over the place, but fear, anger, and hopelessness stood as mighty foes that attacked and dominated me, making me their captive. I sat there lost in my mind but at the same time thinking, *Will this be the sum of my existence? Will all people remember of me is that I went crazy? If this stage of my life is only temporary, when will I find relief?*" I had so many questions but never any answers, or so I thought.

Even though my mouth never cried out to God, what I didn't understand was that my heart never stopped screaming for Him and deliverance. The night I left Tunisia's house, I felt like life was over. I had hurt, scared, and disrespected the one person in my life who stayed in my corner, and so hopelessness clung to me like sap to a maple tree. However, that night was the beginning of my journey back to sanity.

Once I was back on my meds, the therapists felt I was safe to go back into the world, but I had nowhere to go. They brought me back to the hospital to await an open bed at a nursing home. It took the hospital one week to find a bed for me in Oakland.

Chapter 7

The Birth of Light

I arrived at the Sunnyside nursing care facility on December 14, 2006. For three weeks, I stayed to myself and quietly struggled with the voices in my head. On the second day of the fourth week, I met a man named Randy Street. Randy was a 300-pound, dark skinned, black man about 50 years old. He had one withered armed and rode a power scooter. Randy and I started to hang out, smoke cigarettes together, and talk. Our friendship helped me to focus on the reality of this world and not the reality of my mind. I slowly slipped back into this world. The nursing home was a boring existence, so Randy often left and went outside. Somehow the doctor had cleared him to leave, but he had to be back before dark. While he was out, I wandered through the hallways searching for something, but I didn't know what.

I found what I was looking for in room 34, bed number 2, and his name was James. James was a sixty-eight-year-old African American man with a dark skin tone who often bragged about being a singer in his youth. No one ever believed him until a new nurse produced a CD that clearly showed him on the cover. James and I began to talk when Randy was out. James was in a car accident at the age of thirty-five when he was at the top of his music career. He said the accident took everything he held dear, and like me, he lost the use of his legs. I could not tell his secret thoughts or how long it took him to come to grips with his situation, but one thing was clear—he now cherished being alive. James taught me no matter what the situation of life, if you look closely enough, there is always beauty at its core. As I searched for the beauty, I found my son Vonne.

I began to call Vonne every day, and slowly we started to mend our relationship, which caused a longing in my soul. I longed to see him, to be a dad to him, and to guide him during his young years. This longing dominated my every thought until it became a goal of life for me. I often envisioned myself in my own apartment taking care of Vonne and continually dreamed of that day. The opportunity presented itself for me to do just that in the spring of 2007. Randy and the counselor of the nursing home had been searching for an apartment for him. They found a cheap room in West Oakland whose manager was willing to accept him. When Randy found out he was leaving, he urged me to follow him, and he would watch over me. Every day leading up to Randy's departure, I talked to people about the area and building. Some people had good things to say, and others said bad things, but it was the words of the maintenance man that help me make my decision. He said, "Anywhere you go, there will be good and bad people, but if you stay to yourself and not let them in your house, you'll be okay."

Armed with this advice, I began plotting my freedom from the home.

The first thing was to get the doctors to clear me to leave. I started to comply with everything that was asked of me. Although this helped with the attitudes of the nurses, it didn't go very far with the doctors. Each time I would see a doctor, I would ask, "How am I doing?"

They all would say, "You're doing good. You will be out of here in no time."

However, no one would say when that would be, so one day I just asked, "Can I go to the apartment building that Randy went to?"

The doctor was surprised that I was thinking of leaving. "Do you think you're ready to be on your own?"

I said, "Yeah, I've been thinking about it a lot and I'm ready."

"If you could remember to ask the nurse for your meds before she brings them to you, then we both will believe you're ready."

That gave me hope. "Thank you. I'll do it. Watch and see."

The possibility that I might have a chance to leave and have an apartment of my own was exhilarating, and so I never stopped thinking of it. The next day, I was up before sunrise, and at 7:00 AM I went to the nurse's station and asked for my meds. She smiled. "I wish you the best, but I won't remind you, okay?"

I smiled back. "I'll remember."

She went to the chart and proceeded to give me my meds. I took them and rolled off to go tell Randy the good news. The day the doctor told me I might be going home, Randy was out and didn't return on time, so I fell asleep. However, the next morning, I couldn't wait to see him. Since he didn't come to breakfast, I went straight to his room and shook him awake.

I said, "Guess who might be going to the building after you?"

Randy rolled over and asked, "Who?"

I said, "Yo, patna the doctor told me if I can remember to ask for my meds before the nurse brings them to me, I can leave in two weeks."

Randy sat up and said, "We gon' have a good time! You don't have to worry about nothing, I got you."

I made it through the two weeks perfectly. Many of the nurses were happy not just because I had done it. They said, "We were getting tired of you bugging us."

I had to wait three extra days to see the doctor, which felt more like a year. Once I saw him, he smiled and said, "Not one miss. How'd you do it? I guess love is a strong motivator, huh? Frederick, I talked to your son's mother, and she said you want to get out of here so you can see your son on a more regular basis. I think that's great, but if you slip, all that you have worked so hard for would be gone, so please don't slip."

I smiled. "I don't ever want to be in a place like this ever again, so you don't have to worry about me." That day the doctor cleared me to leave, but at the time I had only known of the apartment building but never talked to anyone there. I couldn't call on my own, so I had to wait on the counselor. After the doctor released me, I was at her door every day, but the wheels of progress move slowly, or in her case very, very slowly. In her defense, she was the only counselor for the 150 patients at the facility. She finally called me in two weeks later. I was excited and ready to go, but she laid out a plan that would have taken two months, and my mouth dropped. I left her office depressed, so when Randy saw me, he knew something was wrong. As I told him what the counselor told me, he laughed.

I didn't know what was so funny, and my depression grew, but then he said, "Look, all you have to do is call this number and ask to speak to the manager."

I said, "I can't. She said I got to wait on her."

He said smugly, "Then it will take two months or longer."

"Wait, what's that number?" I asked.

I made the first call to the manager of the apartment building on a Monday, and exactly four weeks later, I was in my own apartment. Richie and Kim somehow knew I was leaving, so they came to help me move. They came and took the keys and decorated the apartment for me. Richie even gave me a blanket he bought while on his military deployment in Iraq, which I cherished. When I arrived at the apartment and settled in, I told Richie, "I don't like it; it's too small."

Richie said, "Tootie, it's yours. You don't have to worry about anyone or anything. You can come in here, close the world out, and have peace. This is all you need."

After his talk I felt better about the place and asked him, "Richie, do you have a TV I could use?"

He said, "I'll bring you one tomorrow." As he turned to leave, I felt a sadness that can only be compared to how a child feels when their parents leave them on their first day at school.

However, true to his word, Randy was at my door bright and early the next morning asking if I wanted to go get something to eat. Randy became my best friend, and we spent most of our time sitting in front of the building smoking weed and sipping on alcohol. Before I met Randy, I never wanted the company of someone in a wheelchair or power scooter because it reminded me of my condition. However, I felt no problem being with him riding up and down the streets of Oakland. Our relationship blossomed over the next three years. I never tried to get over on him, and I protected him from those who sought to use him. Randy was a very intelligent man, but he could not read, write, or do math very well; his knowledge was of the world, and it was based on common sense.

He was one who desperately clung to his independence. He allowed no one to speak for him or write his papers. When he had to write something, he used the dictionary and very simple words, but he did it, and of that he was proud. He began to trust me, and for him that was amazing. In his fifty-three years, he had often run into people who used him and took advantage of his kindness, which made him distrustful of others. Randy once told me of a time when he was young and told his mom that he trusted her. She told him not to trust her because one day she might let him down, so he should only trust himself. This advice Randy took to heart and lived by it for most of his life, but I guess he saw I only wanted the best for him.

Randy's limitations with education made him idolize me as I excelled in the things he suffered at. Due to the fact that Randy could not do math, he often gave out more money than he wanted to. Many times, he mistakenly gave me a fifty instead of the twenty he was supposed to. So I became his human calculator. When he needed to add something up or pay a person for something, he would call me to add up the figures and tell him how much to pay. Randy was my hero: he had so much to complain about, but I never heard him do so. He took everything and worked with what he had. Most forget that it is not a given to have two hands or two feet and a brain that works right until they don't have it or can't use it anymore. In his youth, Randy did a lot of drugs and messed up his lungs, so he was in and out of the hospital. That left me alone in the building a lot, which caused me to look for other friends to hang out with.

The Relationship

In the fall of 2005, a young African American woman moved into the building, and not just into the building but directly across from my apartment. At the time, Randy and I started to sell drugs in front of the building and were making good money. But I was lonely and sought the companionship of a woman. I tried to meet the young lady, whose name was Dianna, but all she offered was a brief conversation one late night, and the rest of the time she ignored me. As a result, I didn't give her much thought until late one night she knocked on my door. Opening the door, I could not believe what my eyes saw. There she stood, all 5'5" of her, with the most beautiful dark complexion, light brown eyes, and perfectly shaped body. I couldn't get the words out right, so I just looked and smiled. She must have seen that I was stuck, so she asked, "Can I come in?"

I said, "Yeah, come on in."

"Can I sit on your bed?"

"Yeah, go ahead."

She began to flirt and talk to me so I responded, but I was lost in her beauty. She asked, "What's your name? Do your stereo work?"

"My name is Fred," I answered. "And yeah, it works. Why do you ask?"

She said, "I have a lot of music. I'll be right back."

She left and went across the hall to her apartment. When she returned, she was carrying a big box full of CDs. She went straight for the stereo and put on a song by R. Kelly. The song she played was "I'm a Flirt," and not long after she began to dance in a mirror I had sitting against the wall. I watched as she bounced and twisted her body to the music and thought of how she would look naked. We sat, talked, and drank alcohol until the early morning. At about 2:30 AM she decided to go home, but not before she asked for my phone number. As she walked out the door, I said to myself, "I would love to have her for my woman." She called my phone ten minutes later and asked me to come to her house.

When I entered her house, she was lying on her bed in a tight leather skirt. She looked me in the eyes and said, "Let's do something."

Since it had been years since I approached or had a woman proposition me, I asked, "Do what?"

She said, "You know what I mean."

It hit me like a ton of bricks. She wanted to sleep with me, but for some reason I couldn't bring myself to get into her bed, so I said, "I can't."

She then said, "Well, give me a kiss then."

I slowly bent over to kiss her, and as she leaned in closer, I closed my eyes and our lips met. I couldn't believe it. Here I was kissing the woman that every man in the building was talking about. As I pulled away, she laid her head on the pillow and passed out. I sat there staring at the roundness of her butt. I couldn't help myself, so I slowly ran my hand back and forth on it. She didn't move, but I started to feel like a pervert, so I stopped. I left a note and then I left my keys, took hers, and locked her in the apartment. I thought for sure I had blown it. Here she was basically throwing herself at me, and I rejected all of her advances. But the next day, I awoke to her standing over me wearing a big smile.

She said, "Fred, I have never had a person reject me when I offered sex to them. But you know what, I kinda felt honored that you didn't take advantage of me." After that night, she stuck by my side. We took turns spending the night at each other's house.

While she never minded coming to my apartment, I kind of like hers better. It looked and felt more homey. Dianna's house had the most beautiful red and tan curtains that matched her bedspread. There were red candleholders that hung from golden stands sitting on both of her dressers. She hung pictures on her walls, but unlike the picture frames that hung on mine, hers were color coordinated. She never used the overhead lights; instead, she had a dimly lit lamp in the corner of her apartment that set the mood. She loved me, and even though I couldn't understand why, I loved that she always wanted me around.

I juggled my time between Randy and Dianna for the better part of two years. Randy never tripped because he felt sorry for me. One day as we sat in front of the building, I was bragging about Dianna's love for me and our sex life when Randy said something that bothered me for four years. After I was finished bragging, Randy said, "Better you than me."

As soon as the words registered in my mind, I thought, "Why would he say that?" Here I was living the dream of most men my age. I had a beautiful twenty-three-year-old young lady who loved me and my sex, had a job, her own apartment, and no kids, so I thought, "Who wouldn't want this life?" I never asked Randy why he said those words, but time often brings with it knowledge if you pay close attention, and observation was one of my stronger attributes.

Dianna and I spent most of our time in her apartment drinking, listening to music, and having sex. I thought I was in love with her, but I truly didn't know what love really was. I cherished her and tried to give her the world. She never asked me for anything but beer, but all she had to do was mention something she could use, and I would run to get it. She always told me all she wanted was my time, but I just kept buying her things. I was what the hood would call sprung, nose wide opened, or walking blind and naked. That would have been ok if she didn't have a drinking problem. Although she loved me, the alcohol caused her to act out and constantly start arguments with me. For the most part, she told me the right thing to do, but it was me who chose the bad. And being with her made the bad choice easier to choose.

As time passed, I slowly started to change. I can't say when it started, but I knew something was different. Before I met Dianna, I wasn't selling, using drugs, or drinking every day, but after only a few months, I was doing all three. To keep up with my spending habits, I started to supplement my income by selling drugs. I sold weed, pills, and crack cocaine, and also during this time I started to snort powder cocaine. Without even knowing it, I had slipped back into darkness. One night as I sat in my room bagging up crack with a plate of weed sitting on the TV and twenty ecstasy pills on my bed, I thought, "What the hell are you doing?" I started to trace back what had kicked off the change. The only thing that kept coming to my mind was that it was her. Even with that knowledge, I still stayed in the relationship with her, until I realized what it was doing to Vonne.

Vonne was suffering in silence. He was seeking my attention, and I was devoting all my time to Dianna. Before she entered into the picture, Vonne and I used to have dad and son talks at least once a week. What I found out was he was greatly missing these talks. One day while Dianna was at work and Vonne was with me at the house, we started to talk.

I asked him, "What's up, Vonne?"

He responded, "I'm having a tough time with my mom."

"Why?"

"She always on my back."

"What are you doing that's causing her to be?"

"Well, Dad, me and a friend was out playing and we accidentally hit a car while having a rock fight. She totally overreacted, Dad. It wasn't like I meant to do it or there was a lot of damage or anything, but she whipped me and grounded me for two weeks."

I asked, "Vonne, were you thinking?"

He first said, "Yeah." Then I guess he thought about the question and asked, "What do you mean was I thinking?"

I asked, "Where were y'all when y'all was throwing rocks?"

"We were on San Pablo Dam Road."

"Was that a smart thing to do seeing that there is a freeway off ramp on that street?"

He shrugged. "Dad, how was I to know that?

"Didn't you see all the cars going up and down on the street?

"Yeah," He admitted.

I asked, "So even after you recognized all the cars, you still thought it okay to throw rocks? Vonne, were you thinking?"

He said, "Yeah, we weren't throwing them at the cars."

I shook my head. "No, Vonne, you weren't thinking. If you had, you would have thought of the consequences of your actions, three of which happened.

You did hit a car, and you were punished. That's it. You don't get to choose or say what an appropriate response to your bad judgement should be.

"The only thing you can choose is what action you will take and that choice if for the good will produce good, but if you choose to make a bad choice, as you did in that situation, then as you found out, it will produce bad for you. So, you have to think every choice through to the end and see all that could happen and choose right. That way you'll only reap the good."

"My bad, Dad," He said. "I'll tell my mom I'm sorry for getting upset at her."

"That would be a smart thing to do."

As we sat there talking, I said to him "Man, Vonne, it seems like we ain't done this in a long time."

He responded, "Yeah, Dad, it's been a year since we had one of our talks."

"A year? That's a long time. Are you sure?"

"Yeah, Dad, I'm sure."

I was taken aback. "Vonne, I'm sorry, but when you get older you'll understand why I like spending time with her, but I promise that I will start today to back up from her. I just can't leave right now because my feelings are involved, but know I'm leaving her."

That night I didn't spend the night at Dianna's house but stayed with Vonne. She called all night trying to bribe me with sex, and although I liked making love to her, I loved Vonne more and stayed in my house with him.

The next morning, I looked at her differently. In the beginning I looked upon her as a gift from God, but now all I could see was a distraction that caused me to neglect my son. I stopped having sex and spending so much time with her. After two weeks, I was strong enough to tell her I didn't want to be in a relationship anymore. She was totally caught off guard and didn't see it coming. She asked me why, and I told her I need to be with my son and I can't do both. She was heartbroken and asked me to stay, but I refused. After that conversation we stopped having sex, but I still couldn't bring myself to walk away totally—so we became friends. When Vonne wasn't there, we talked on the phone, and sometimes she spent the night at my house. With Dianna slowly drifting away, I was once again alone and searching for direction. By this time, Randy was in jail, the feelings I had for Diana had fully left my mind, and I was addicted to heroin and lost.

Chapter 8

The Desire to Change

In the end, I hated heroin. At first, it made me feel like the king of the world, and Dianna and I always had the best sex when I was on it. But I began to hate going to get it, I hated doing it every day, and I hated the pain that came if I didn't have it. There was nothing I liked about it, but I just didn't know how to stop. During this time, my friend Edward started to go to a church in Berkeley, California, and he would often come and tell me about the pastor's sermon. After two or three talks, I wanted to hear this pastor for myself. The night of April 3, 2007, I went to Bible study and was instantly captured by the Word of God.

Soon I joined the church and started to attend on a regular basis. I had never been in a church to hear the word in my thirty-five years of life. I went to a church named Glide Memorial Church in downtown San Francisco as a child, but I don't remember ever hearing the Word. I also attended some services at Peniel, but all I could remember was the one scripture I had to remember in order to play basketball. I loved this new church. Every sermon made me feel as if the pastor were talking directly to me. One day after sitting through church, the pastor asked, "Is there anyone here who would like to be baptized?" Slowly, I started down the walkway until I was sitting in front of the pastor. He lifted up his hands and said, "Thank the Lord, we have one soul seeking forgiveness." I didn't really understand what baptism was, but I knew I needed to have it done.

The baptism was scheduled for the next Sunday service, and I eagerly awaited it... until the dreams started. I invited my whole family to come and watch, but all had other plans except for my older sister Kim. My anticipation for the baptism was eclipsed by my fear because for some strange reason I started to have nightmares about the baptism. It was as if something didn't want me to do it. My nightmares were incomprehensible, and I didn't speak about them to others. The first dream was of me standing in a flaming circle with what appeared to be a snake wrapping itself around my legs. I desperately tried to free myself, but it hung on no matter what I did or how hard I fought.

My next dream was the scariest. I was in a city, and it was full of thugs who were chasing me. I ran into an abandoned building to hide, but they found me and started to ask me questions. Many of them stood around laughing until the leader pulled out a gun; even in my dream, I felt fear. As I stood there not knowing what to say or why I was there, he looked me in the eye and then shot me in the face. I awoke with sweat falling down my face and fear running through my spine. The night before the baptism, Kim came to spend the night at my house so she could be there to support me. We sat together smoking cigarettes and talking.

I told her, "Kim, I'm not sure if I want to get baptized anymore."

She asked, "Why?"

"I don't know. I just feel that something will go wrong."

"Why did you want to be baptized in the first place?" She asked.

I said, "Because I just want to be with God and do whatever He wants me to do."

"Do you still feel that way?"

"Yeah."

"Well then, Tootie, you know what you should do, right?"

I nodded. "Yeah—get baptized."

She said, "There you have it. Don't worry, I'll be there to help you if you start to drown." As she hit her cigarette and gave me a crooked smile, I smiled back at her, and from that point on I was sure of my decision. The day of the baptism brought with it joy and uncertainty, but also an expectation that hasn't been matched since that day. I was the first in the shower and dressed. Kim took her time as women often do, but it was extremely irritating because I was ready to go.

I began to say, "Kim, hurry up."

She kept telling me, "Tootie, the church ain't going nowhere—just wait."

Once she was dressed, we started for the bus stop but made a detour to get our coffee.

As we waited for the bus she asked, "Tootie, are you sure you want to do this?"

I said, "Yeah. I just want to do God's will, and I believe this is the first step."

We were silent the whole bus ride, but the silence was broken on the walk to the church. Kim asked, "Tootie, how they gon' get you in the water seeing you can't walk?"

I had never thought about that, but now it dominated my thoughts the rest of the way to the church. Once we arrived, I went straight to the pastor and asked how he was going to get me to the water. The pastor was a young African American man of about thirty with dark skin and a warm disposition. He looked down at me and said, "Fred, it's God's will for you to be baptized today, so don't worry. He has already prepared the way."

I still wasn't satisfied, but I had to take his word for it. As I made my way to my spot, the music started to play, signaling the start of worship. The pastor grabbed the mic and began to sing, "Pass me not, oh gentle Savior. Hear my humble cry. While on others thou art calling, do not pass me by." The song really set the mood and placed us in the spirit of worship.

After he was done, he prayed, "God, we humble ourselves before thee and ask that You fill this place with thy Spirit." The pastor then asked, "Will the baptismal participant please stand or raise your hands in the sight of God to be acknowledge?"

After this was done, he asked us to leave the room and get ready for our baptism. The church had prepared a room for me to get undressed, and Kim accompanied me to help me change into the gown.

As Kim and I entered the room, she asked one last time, "Tootie, is this what you truly want?"

I replied, "Yeah."

She said, "Then I'm glad to share this day with you."

I turned and gave her a hug. "Thank you, Kim. I wouldn't want anyone else here."

She smiled. "You better hurry up or they gon' pass you up."

I smiled back. "If they do I'm flashing" (getting mad).

When I rolled out of the room, the pastor was baptizing the first of four people. As they walked up to the water, he gave a little speech about the person. For each person it was something different, but it made a lasting impression on the congregation. When it was my turn, I rolled up to the pulpit and sat in front of the stairs. The pastor asked for two angels (or helpers) from the crowd to come forth. Two of the deacons came up and stood by my chair. They were each about six feet or taller and weighed over two fifty. Once I started to get out of the chair, they came close, one on each side, and grabbed my arms. The walk to the water was a struggle, but the speech the pastor gave was inspirational. He shouted to the congregation, "Look at how he struggles to the water. He will not be denied. The water of life is calling out to him, and he is answering."

As he spoke, one by one the people started to stand until the whole church was on its feet. The two men on the sides of me kept saying, "Just a little more. You got it; just keep walking." The struggle to the pool made me tired, but as the pastor said, I would not be denied, so I gained strength. Once in the water, I stood looking out over the church. Seeing the congregation standing and clapping, I felt as if God were also rejoicing. Entering the pool and standing by my side, the pastor told me to place my hands on his wrist. Then he took the mic and shouted, "In the name of the Father, Son, and Holy Spirit I baptize thee." Then he quickly dunked me under the water and brought me back to a standing position. When I came up out of the water, I felt different. I can't explain it, but it just all felt different. Even the walk back to my chair was easier—I was soaked from the head down and only had one man helping me, but I made it back to the chair quicker and easier than I had made it to the pool. I thought that my life would be easier after the baptism, but it became a harder struggle.

Once I made it back home, the struggle for life began. Before the baptism, I never gave thought to my actions or character, but now I was recognizing the defects. I saw greed, pride, anger, and lust in a new light, and my character was full of all four. I tried not to think about it, but the Spirit opened my eyes and began to change my motives. However, evil was also close by my side to tempt me to partake of its pleasures. After my baptism, I was never fully on one side or the other but walked a tight rope between both until I met a man named Michael.

In February of 2008, as I sat in front of my apartment building, Mike walked up to me and started to speak of God. Mike was a short, dark-skinned young man who loved the Lord. He didn't wear the clothes of the day. Instead he wore slacks, collared shirts, loafers, and an old fedora hat. He spoke to me about the Sabbath of the Lord and how God's grace is for everyone. I was instantly drawn into the conversation and started to debate with him over what day we should go to church. After only a few seconds, I knew I was out of my league—he knew way more about God's Word than I did. So I just started to listen, and before we finished our conversation, he told me to ask my pastor what day the true Sabbath was, and I said I would.

That Wednesday at Bible study before the pastor started to teach, he asked, "Do anyone have any questions?"

I raised my hand.

Once he called on me I asked, "What day is the Sabbath of the Lord?"

He said, "Saturday is the seventh day of our week, so if we were to observe the Jewish Sabbath, it would be Saturday."

A lady across from me raised her hand and asked, "If Saturday is the Sabbath, then why do we go to church on Sunday?"

The pastor turned to approach the chalkboard and said, "Here you have to be careful." He began to talk about the crucifixion. "Christ lay in the grave for three days and this is symbolic of the darkness of the world before he came," He said. "He rose to a new life, and so did the world, and because of this we rest in what He has done. Therefore, today we observe Sunday as remembrance of His resurrection."

I didn't ask another question, but I wasn't convinced by his explanation and purposed in my heart to find Mike and see what else he knew. The next morning, I was up early and outside waiting for Mike to pass by the building. At about 12:00 PM, I saw him walking up 34th Street.

I gave chase and told him, "Mike, you were right; The pastor said the Sabbath was on Saturday."

Mike said, "I told you, Fred."

I said, "I would like to know more if you have time."

He responded, "Fred, we can have a Bible study if you up for it."

"Sure, when is it good for you because I'm free anytime."

"I'll be at your house tomorrow at 10:00 AM so be up, all right?"

"All right, I'll see you later."

During my thirty-five years on this earth, I had never read the Bible or thought of God as a Helper, Redeemer, or as loving me. From the age of sixteen I chose to go it alone, and I had to take care of myself. If I needed something, it was on me to make it happen. I liked smoking, drinking, and getting money, and I didn't want to stop. At the time, Dianna and I were off and on, and my kids' moms were letting them come to see me more. I always needed to keep a few dollars on hand just in case my kids needed it, so I kept selling drugs. Since my baptism, I began thinking more of the future and my final end. My eyes were soon to be opened to the reality of God, His laws, and my responsibility as a Christian through Mike's teaching.

The next morning, Mike was at my door at 10:00 AM sharp. He brought with him two Bibles and two purplish books that we were to study out of. As he sat on my bed, he handed me the purple book and asked, "Do you see anything in this book that you would like to study?"

I said, "Yeah, let's study about the Sabbath."

"All right, go to page 25."

In just four short pages, I learned more about God than I had known my entire life. I learned that God has laws that are called the Ten Commandments. In this law, God commands humans to rest on the seventh day as He rested on the seventh day of creation. I also learned that the reason most people go to church on Sunday is entrenched in contemporary tradition rather than biblical principles or laws. Specifically, the Roman Catholic Church changed the holiness and observance of the Sabbath from Saturday to Sunday. They claimed that

God conferred with the Pope and gave His permission for the Pope to change the day of worship. But nowhere in the Bible does it state that there is another day that we are to worship God. I was like a child with a new toy because all I wanted to do was read and tell someone of the love of God. So, Mike and I took to the streets with God's message of love.

Our hearts burned within us to speak, and the joy of forgiveness invigorated our every step as we marched. Each morning, we met at Mike's house and planned our attack. First, we chose to minister in our own neighborhood. Mike knew a man who would supply all the materials we needed. Our materials were mostly books, leaflets, and handbills. As we marched, we developed a fight song that we shouted out loud as we walked. Our song was very simple but effective. I started by yelling, "God is good all the time," then Mike yelled, "And all the time God is good." We yelled this message so much that some days people who heard us coming shouted it back to us. After proselytizing in our neighborhood, we took the message towards Richmond, California.

We were preaching in many neighborhoods, but we encountered difficulties and resistance along the way, so I was confused and saddened. We met like any other day, and our spirits were as blissful and flaming as all the other days, but the field was not ripe to harvest. No one received our message, and at every turn people declined to take the material. Mike had already met the spirit of resistance before and was unshaken, but I took it as a personal rejection. We walked through three cities, starting at 34th Street and San Pablo Avenue in Oakland, California, to Albany, California. We still had half of our material left. Furthermore, Mike's feet were hurting, so we decided to turn around and head back home. Along the way home, Mike and I began to discuss what had happened that day. As I spoke of the confusion that was plaguing my mind, Mike interrupted me.

He said, "Fred, they not rejecting you; they're rejecting Christ, because it's His message."

I said, "I know, but it hurts. It's like they think the devil is going to win the battle."

Mike laughed. "Fred, why do you think that?"

"We're out here giving them an opportunity to join the winning team, but they're refusing. The only reason I could think of is they think Christ is really the loser, and no one wants to join a losing team."

Mike bursted out laughing. "Fred, these people don't think that. Most don't think of God at all. They're too busy with the cares of life, the deceitfulness of riches, or they just believe the lie of evolution."

This didn't cure the sadness I felt, but I knew it was probably the truth.

The bus came not much after this conversation, and as we boarded, we could hear a man yelling. He was sitting right next to the wheelchair, so Mike came and stood close to me. I can't remember who said what first, but somehow, we started talking about God with this man. As we went deeper into the conversation, I noticed that this man was slowly turning the conversation away from God to aliens. The man kept saying that mankind was a creation of aliens, and he used the ancient Egyptian civilization to support his ideas. We opened up the Bible and began to try to teach him, but he just got all the louder, so we let him talk. By this time, Mike had already decided that it would be pointless to keep trying to voice our opinions, so he counseled me to stop answering him. The bus pulled up to our stop in no time, and as the doors opened, the man yelled, "Get out of here Satan."

We laughed but said nothing.

Although Mike and I were doing God's work, we were constantly bumping heads. The experience we shared that day would be one of the last times we would be together ministering because although Mike and I were doing God's work, we were constantly bumping heads.

Mike was a passionate person when it came to God and His laws. Because of this, we never saw eye to eye. Mike believed in showing a person the error of his ways, and I had many errors in my life at that time. Mike would often show me scriptures that convicted me, but I still didn't want to change. So, we clashed. I made up excuses why I couldn't change, and he kept trying to remind me that with God all things are possible. We argued back and forth until Mike had enough and was silent. Around this time, Mike was also involved with a couple of other young men who were setting up pastors from other cities to come to Oakland to speak. We drifted apart, and I was left alone to find my way.

The Ministry

For two months, I tried to get Mike to come out and minister with me. He was always too busy, so I went alone. At first, I was afraid because I was unsure of myself spiritually. I read a lot and wrote sermonettes, but I had no one to speak them to—until one day a thought ran through my mind: go preach at the BART station. That night, I developed ten questions and used Bible scriptures to answer them. I used questions like, "How can a young man cleanse his way? By taking heed unto the word of God." I decided to go to the small business courtyard near Fruitvale BART station in East Oakland and just yell out the questions and answers over and over again. I arrived at the station at 9:00 AM and stayed until 2:00 PM. No crowd ever formed to hear me, but it was as if one had, because I was happy doing it all the same. I went to the courtyard near the BART station for two months until the security guards told me the business owner didn't want people hanging out in the courtyard. I was disappointed, but the love of preaching had taken hold of me, so I looked for other opportunities.

Once again, I heard a still small voice within say, "Go preach at nursing homes." I obeyed and that night looked up nursing homes in Oakland. Finding three of them only a bus ride away from my house, I became determined to go there in the morning. I called ahead and made an appointment with the activities director of the home.

I arrived ten minutes early and waited. As I sat, one resident came up to me and asked, "Who are you?"

I said, "My name is Frederick."

"Who you come to see?" He asked.

I responded, "I'm here to see Dee. I'm trying to come here and preach the word of God to y'all."

He smiled. "Oh, you a minister? I was a pastor for thirty years, so you better know what you talking about."

"If I don't, I hope you will help me out," I answered.

As he smiled, Dee called me in.

Dee was a young Asian woman of about twenty-five with long, flowing jet-black hair. She stood about 5'1" and had a caramel complexion. As we talked, I could see she really cared about the residents because as the many residents came to her door, she gave each one the time they needed even though we were in a meeting.

She only asked me five questions. The first was: "What do you plan on doing here?"

I stated, "I want to preach the word of God to the residents and maybe hold one-on-one Bible studies."

She asked, "What denomination are you?"

"Seventh Day Adventist. My home church is Market Street Church in West Oakland."

"Are you going to be preaching about judgment and hell?"

"No," I answered. "I'm here to preach the love of God and salvation. Hell is a good motivator for some, but God wants us to love him not fear him. People make the mistake of telling people of the fear of God without the mercy of God, which causes people to turn from God. My job is to lead men and women to the Cross and help them to see the love in His death."

She nodded. "Good; we had a man preaching that stuff, and it gave the residents nightmares, so we had to let him go."

I said, "God wishes that none should perish, but that all should come to repentance. This is what my studies will focus on."

She turned the conversation to the residents and asked, "Have you had much experience dealing with older people? They can be sweet but also difficult at the same time, and one needs a lot of understanding, patience, and love when dealing with them."

I said, "They sound a lot like my kids. If I can deal with my kids, I think I can handle it, but if something arises, I'll come to you."

Her last question was, "When would you like to start?"

"I can be here tomorrow at 10:00 AM."

"Sounds good. I'll see you then."

That night I prayed and asked God to give me a message to speak to the people in the morning. I opened up the Word and started to read. My message developed very slowly, but at about midnight I was done, so I went to sleep. I awoke at six thirty in the morning full of excitement. While I was getting dressed, I wondered if anyone would want a Bible study or if I would be going for nothing. I arrived five minutes early and started to ask the residents if anyone wanted to sit and go through the Bible, but no one did. Then Dee came into the lounge and asked, "Frederick, would you follow me?"

I didn't say a word. I just started for the door. We walked through the hallways until we arrived at the cafeteria. Once I walked through the door, I noticed that most of the residents of the home were seated in the room. However, what I didn't notice was that they were waiting on me. Before that day, I had never spoke in front of a crowd, and when I awoke that morning, I had not planned on starting that day. Dee went straight to the front of the crowd and started to introduce me. She said, "Hello everybody, today we have a speaker who will be bringing the Word of God, so give him your undivided attention." Then she turned to me and said, "Frederick, they're all yours."

I was shocked, terrified, and excited all at once, but I started to the front of the room praying for strength and clarity. As I turned to face the crowd, all the fear, anxiety, and doubt flew away like leaves from a tree in the winter months.

I looked down at the papers in my hands, then at the crowd, then I opened my mouth and began to teach. I started with some questions, "What is justification? How can we obtain it?" Six or seven of the residents raised their hands to give answers. I called on an older black woman who was sitting close to the door. Sitting in a manual wheelchair, she had a head full of grayish white hair and big-rimmed glasses.

She stated, "To be justified is the act of being right with God, and the only way to gain it is through Jesus Christ."

I said, "That's right, young lady. I'm here today to speak to y'all of the Gift of God in Christ."

That day, in just one moment, I found love. I found love for other people's souls, love for the Word of God, love of preaching, and love for God through the gift of helping others. I learned that my problems are only as big as I make them, and the way to forget them is through helping others. The crowd listened intently and at times asked questions. The give and take that happened as I spoke was like nothing I had ever experienced. It drew me in and filled me with excitement. *I felt as if I had been tottering on the precipice of life, and as a leaf sways in the wind, so was I caressed by the breath of the Spirit of God.* There was a sense of being that has led me to seek out those who need help and try to supply their needs in each step of my life since then. As I stood at the bus stop wondering what just happened and asking myself how I could replicate the experience, I turned and lit up a cigarette.

At the time I had only two cigarettes, but I smoked the first one, and as I dropped it I heard a still small voice say within me, "We not buying no more cigarettes." I smoked the last one, and by the time it was done, the bus was just pulling up. As I got on the bus, I looked back at the butts on the ground and wondered if they were really my last cigarettes. When I got to my stop, I rolled off the bus with no more desire to smoke. Once I entered my house, I got undressed, got in bed, and started to read my Bible. As I think back, the only time the thought of a cigarette came to mind was in the morning. Waking up, I started to look around on the bed for my pack. Realizing there was none to find, I just reminded myself that I didn't smoke, and that was that. I had conquered that situation and habit, but there was still my addiction to heroin that was holding me back.

Each morning I awoke to the realization that my body was craving something that, in reality, was killing me. I partook of it three times a day no matter where I was or what I was doing. Whether at home, school, or even in church, I would have to step away to take my noonday shot of the drug. Although I did it, my heart was constantly crying out for change—but I didn't have the strength to overcome it in my own power. While in church three weeks after I overcame the cigarettes, my victory came. That day started as every other day did: with me in the bathroom cooking up my two shots of heroin. After I cooked them up and drew them into the needles, I took my morning shot, placed the other needle in my sock, and started for church. Little did I know that this day would turn into a day that was unlike any day I have ever lived up to that date. As I entered the church, a feeling of disgust came over me. I didn't understand it because this was not the first time I had come to church high, but it was the first time I saw myself with truthful eyes. It was not pretty because I saw myself as a sinner, and not just that. I asked myself the hard question: "Are you a Christian?" The answer was "NO!" How could I be high and expect to hear the voice of God? The truth is a dangerous thing to someone who truly wants to change, because it brings you face to face with your deformity.

Now faced with the truth of my actions and spiritual death, I started to cry out to God. As I sat in my chair in the corner of the church crying and praying for help, God sent an angel to me in the form of an elder of the church.

He stood at the top of the stairs and asked, "Frederick, are you all right?"

I said, "No, I'm hurting."

He started down the stairs and sat by me. "What's the problem?"

I looked him in the eyes and said, "You know what I've been asking people to pray for."

"No, what is it?"

"Elder, I'm addicted to drugs! Heroin has me, and I can't let it go."

He looked up at me and said, "Let's pray."

He stuck out his hand for me to grab, and I did, but as he prayed, my sadness turned to joy and assurance. When I closed my eyes, I was at the point of desperation and felt the enormity of my emptiness. When I lifted my eyes up, it was as if all had changed. I would not fully recognize the significance of that moment until I had been clean for three years. What my mind couldn't understand was that I had been cleansed. When I arrived home that night, the thought came to me that I still had a quarter ounce of the drug in the bottom of my bathroom cabinet. Knowing that I had heroin within reach scared me so badly that I went straight to bed and hid under the covers until I went to sleep. When I awoke, I did not enter the bathroom due to the fact that I was scared of being tempted to do the drug. But after four weeks and no withdrawals, I decided to throw the needles and the bag of drugs in the trash.

What was worse than doing the drug every day was that my kids knew I was doing it. It was a rewarding experience when I was able to show them that I had finally conquered the habit. One day while all the kids were at my house, I looked at Traivonne and said, "Go get that bag out of the bathroom."

He looked at me and asked, "What bag?"

By this time the other kids were dead silent as they stared at Vonne, but I said, "You know what bag

I'm talking about. Go get the bag that I keep that stuff in."

Vonne slowly got up and went into the bathroom, opened up the cabinet under the sink, and brought the bag out into the living room. The other kids sat there looking at us both, then Vonne asked, "What you want me to do with this?" as he held the bag between two fingers and out away from his body as if it contained a deadly virus.

"Come with me, and bring the bag." I opened the front door and started for the back door where the big trashcan was.

Vonne asked again, "What you want me to do with this bag, Dad?"

I said, "Go put it in the trash can."

Vonne looked puzzled. In order to get to the cans, he had to walk down some stairs, so once he did it, he knew even if I wanted it, I could not reach it.

The look on Vonne's face was so gratifying. The abstinence that followed proved to my kids that the power of God was working in my life and that I was serious about turning away from drugs. A year later, Vonne asked how I was able to just walk away from drugs like that; it gave me an opportunity to speak to him about God and the power of prayer.

As I sat in the house reading, Vonne came in and sat on the foot of the bed. "Dad, you really stopped using that drug?"

I said, "Yeah, why you ask? What, you think I'm still on it?"

He said, "No, but I just can't see how you could do it like that. I know older men in the neighborhood that has been using that drug longer than I've been alive, and all of them want to stop."

I said, "Vonne, I can take no credit. I really did nothing to help myself but desire to be clean and seek the power of God to accomplish it."

His response was typical of a child. "Come on, Dad, really? You telling me all you did was pray?"

"Yeah, but not just once: this has been a battle for three years. For the whole three years, I been praying on buses, at the lake, in the house, and every time the situation came to mind. After three years of constant praying, my faith matched my desire, and the power of God was able to work because I believed that it was only through Him that I could be healed. The Bible says that we're saved by grace through faith. So, faith allows grace to work, and my faith in the power of God healed me."

Vonne shrugged. "If you say so, but it's hard to believe."

Although at that time Vonne was not ready to pray or receive God, the lesson stuck. When he was in trouble, he told me that he called out to God for help and saw God work in his favor. Seeing me turning away from drugs was the most influential experience of my kids' young lives. Due to this they may not want God, but they all know where to go when they need what man cannot provide.

Chapter 9

My Pursuit of Knowledge

After I stopped using drugs, I felt as if the darkness was dispelled, and the light was finally shining in my life. I started to see things I had never seen in my life, such as positive role models, and although they were all the religious type, they propelled me to dream. Dreaming had stopped for me at the tender age of ten when I became aware of my family's condition. What replaced it was my corruption, because I had to focus on today, not tomorrow. Now I was seeing men of intelligence, confidence, and good character. I coveted what they had, and I knew that the way to get it was through education.

One day, a thought entered my mind that prompted me to go sign up for school at Merritt College in Oakland, California. I enrolled in classes that would lead to a degree in addiction counseling and were to start the fall of 2009. I went to the admission office to sign up for financial aid, but I was told I needed a high school diploma or proof that I had passed the GED test. At first, I was discouraged, but after a few minutes, I remembered that I had earned my GED in San Jose in the early nineties. After some calls, I located it and paid to have it sent to my house, and I was able to obtain the money to go to school. In that situation, I learned this lesson: *you cannot wait until an opportunity appears to*

*go get what is needed to receive the blessing. You must
already have the tools in your toolbox.* I had the means,
I knew the way, but I lacked the courage.

On the first day of class, as I waited for the bus
that would take me to the school, I started to second-
guess my decision. Looking around at all the young
eighteen- and twenty-year-olds talking and horse playing
with each other, I felt very uncomfortable. I sat there
waiting for the number 54 bus, close to the number 14
bus stop that could have taken me home, and I was
conflicted over which bus to actually catch. The longer I
sat there, the more I felt like going home, so when the
bus that could take me home showed up, I jumped on it,
went home, and dropped my classes. At the time I
thought it was for the best, but as the months passed, I
started to realize that I would have already completed
one semester if I had followed through. The entire four
months that I waited for the next semester to start, I only
focused on the benefit of going to school. This cancelled
out the fear, so when spring rolled around, I was ready to
sign up again. This time instead of Merritt College, I
decided to go to Laney College, which was close to my
house.

In the Spring of 2009, I decided to take a
computer class. I knew I would need to know how to use
one in order to actually be productive in college. The
class was taught by a middle-aged Asian man named Mr.

Chew. He stood about 5'3", was of a thick build, and wore big-rimmed, black framed glasses. He was one of the most patient men I have ever known. Although he was teaching basic computer skills, to us, it was like he was speaking another language. I remember one class where we were supposed to learn how to create and check an email account.

He asked, "How many of you have an email account?"

One older African American woman raised her hand. "I have a post office box that I check every other day."

Mr. Chew just smiled. "That's good, but email is not paper mail; it's mail that comes through and is read on the internet."

While for most of the world, and our kids especially, email was a way of life, most of us in the class didn't even know how to create an email account, let alone check it or send emails. I caught on pretty quickly, but many struggled at the task. However, Mr. Chew took his time with each of us and even offered to help after class and on his lunch break. In his class, we learned how to use email, the internet, and all the programs in Microsoft Office.. I soaked up the information, and after the class was over, I felt prepared to start mainstream classes.

I wanted to take classes in psychology, but once again I was overcome by fear, thinking it would be too hard for me since I had just started. So, for my first four classes I took a basic English, Algebra 1, and two African American history classes. I learned two valuable lessons from my history teacher Mr. Hook and my English teacher Ms. Fuller. Mr. Hook taught us if we were to gain riches through a degree, we would have to learn to conform to what the professional world considered as the norm. With that in mind, he set rules that governed our appearance, language, and actions while we were in his class. His first rule was that young men had to pull up their pants and not wear hats while in the class. Young ladies could not wear pajamas or clothing that was too provocative. We were not to use any foul language or laugh at anyone's comments during his lecture. What had escaped my attention while I in his class became very clear the further along I went in school.

Since we were to act in a professional way, he was training us to lose sight of who we were as African Americans and change our cultural values, morals, and identity to gain respect, riches, and status in the world. With this, Mr. Hook sent me the other way, and instead I learned the opposite of what he wanted us to take away from his class: that my cultural experience mattered and that I would not conform it or deny it, or change it for success. I became determined that through intelligence, determination, and hard work, I would reinvent how an African American man is to be valued, respected, and accepted in the professional world--not in spite of his cultural experience but because of it. For that, the value Ms. Fuller placed on my experience was a breath of fresh air.

Ms. Fuller was an African American woman of about fifty with a brown sugar complexion, thin gold-rimmed glasses, and hair cut short with a touch of grey sprinkled throughout in patches. Her warm spirit, patient disposition, and motivating character pushed me to succeed. Were it not for her advice, this book would not have been possible. Ms. Fuller was very strict when it came to grading our papers, but she made sure to give us the tools to do every assignment to her expectations. All we had to do was remember and use them. Over a three-month period, she explained to the class the format of a good paper. Then she assigned a three-page paper on life experience that paralleled a poem we had studied.

She told us, "I will grade each paper on the things that we have gone over in class. If anyone needs any of the handouts, please stay after class."

I asked, "Can we use any of our experiences even if they may not be something good but show the same lessons learned in the poem?"

She said, "If you learned a lesson from the experience, then it is not bad. It is just a stepping stone that got you here, so yeah, you can use it."

When the class let out and some of us walked together to the student center, along the way we questioned her assignment and complained about the length of the paper. I said, "Dang, she wants three full pages! What the hell we gon' write on for three pages?"

Another young lady chimed in. "She tripping. I'm gonna turn in a page and a half, and that's all she's getting from me."

A young African American kid said, "She only gon' take off a few points, so me too."

But a Latina young lady said, "Hey, it's only three pages. When we get to English 1A we gon' be asked to write eight pages or more, and if you plan to move on, it only gets harder."

I said, "Eight pages? Dang!" But since I did have plans to move on to the next level, I determined to at least try to give her three pages.

When I arrived home, I went straight to work on the paper. I read the poem over again and then meditated on my past and tried to pick a good experience where the lesson I learned matched the poem's message. The author of the poem spoke of the fact that though his upbringing was hard, his childhood slowly helped him develop a silent but overpowering resilience. After looking up what the definition of *resilience* was, I saw many ways in which my childhood matched up with the message. I decided to write about a time when my family was evicted. It took the whole two weeks for me to turn out a paper, but once it was done, I was excited. As I reread my paper, I really thought it was an "A" paper. I felt proud of it and could not wait to turn it in. I had to wait a week to see what she thought of it, but the whole time, I just knew her response was going to be good. However, when the next class came together, Ms. Fuller stood in front of the class and sighed, but I wasn't worried because I thought whatever she had to say wasn't for me. As she stood with all our papers in her hand, she asked the question, "What are the parts that make up an essay?"

No one raised a hand to answer until the quiet Asian young lady in the back of the class who hardly ever spoke did. Ms. Fuller pointed to her and she answered, "An introduction, thesis, topic sentences, body, and a conclusion."

Ms. Fuller said, "Correct, but most of the class didn't follow this simple format. While everybody had very interesting content, most of the papers weren't correctly formatted. Most didn't have topic sentences or flow within their paper, or they left out some part of the structure."

Everyone just sat there; some people rolled their eyes and some smacked their lips in frustration, but we were all anticipating getting our papers back to see what grade we received. As she passed the papers back, she offered everyone the chance to rewrite their papers if they didn't get the grade they were hoping for. As she rounded the back of the class and started for my position, she reached into her left hand to pass me my paper, and I saw a lot of red pen marks on it. She handed it to me upside down, and as I turned it over to see the grade, I was devastated—an F. Not a D or a C, but an F. I instantly raised my hand to ask why she gave me an F, but as I did, she said, "If anyone has any questions about their paper, please wait and stay after class, and we can talk about it then." I sat through the whole class and didn't hear anything: I could not stop thinking about that paper.

After class was over, almost everyone stayed behind, and we spoke to her one at a time. Each time someone went up to the front, the response they had to what she had to say was disappointment and then anger. When it was my turn, I rolled to the front of the class and sat there. Her first words were, "I really enjoyed your paper," which I thought was ironic because she gave me an F.

I asked, "Then why did you give me an F?"

"It was riveting, yes, but it lacked structure and punctuations."

I said, "What?" I was sure she had made a mistake.

She said, "Frederick, you are a very forceful writer, but you need to follow the guidelines of an essay." She then reached into her bag and passed me some papers. "Study these and use the information to rewrite your paper."

She saw that I was really disappointed, so she added, "Hang in there; one paper does not define you. You have what you need to do it right, but it's up to you." As I turned to leave, she said, "Your story was good. It held me, Frederick. I can see you writing a book about your life, but first you need to learn how to write, so I hope you stick with it."

When I left the class, I had an attitude and said to myself, "Watch! I'm gon' show her who can't write." I didn't go to the computer lab where all my friends were, but instead I went straight home and started to rewrite my paper, this time using the handouts as a guide. That night, I learned a lot about myself: I knew I could do a better job, but I had to humble myself. I had to admit I didn't know, and that was hard for me to do. In doing it, I learned one of my most meaningful values: it *takes more strength to admit fear, ignorance, and truth than it does to lie, to act as if I know, and to show anger.*

That F turned out to be an influential part of my growth as a man. As I rewrote the paper, I was also rewriting my understanding of myself and the way I dealt with the world. At the end of the week, I turned in my paper, and a week later I received it back from the teacher. There were still red marks on it, but this time the grade was 100 percent better—a B. She explained the B saying, "I had to take off for you having to rewrite it, Frederick, but overall it was good."

I took one more English class with Ms. Fuller. Through her demanding teaching style, she pushed me to be the best I could be—not just in English but in life as well. Ms. Fuller's classes taught me the value of structure, guidelines, and the understanding that can only be gained through listening. She was the first person who made me realize that my past, although challenging and hard, held value. Not just because I had come through it, but because it could also help others to know they could overcome as well.

She always kept the idea of a book before me. Each time we would see each other on campus, she would ask, "Frederick, when is your book coming out?" She may never know how influential and needed her friendship was in my life. I can honestly say my success, understanding, and growth in academia has its foundation in those first two English classes I took with her. By learning structure and how to follow simple guidelines, I realized that a person's dreams can only be obtained through structure and guidelines. However, it would take time for me to develop the structure I would live by and the methods I would use to follow through with it.

The Test of Friendship

During the 2010 fall semester, I struggled—not because the work was hard but because I was focused on other things. During that time, I had developed a number of friendships, and an old girlfriend named Ashley came back into my life. I started to do things that I had done prior to that time—going out on dates and hanging out with friends after school. Normally, my after-school hours were devoted to study and paper preparation, but I began spending it with others. My papers were done quickly, which produced less than quality work. My study for math quizzes went from three days to one, and I never did the homework, yet I expected high marks for my papers, quizzes, and overall grade. I paid no attention to my lack of effort, but some of my teachers did, and they talked to me. It wasn't until I was faced with a C in math that I woke up.

A math teacher named Racy Damp confronted me and said, "Frederick, you need to get at least an A on both of your remaining quizzes and an A on your final in order to get an A for the class."

I said, "Why? I thought I been doing good in your class."

She said, "You haven't done any homework, and your quizzes have not been in the high percentile. So you are close to getting a B, but in order to earn that A you want, this is what you need to do."

I left that class wondering how I was doing in my other classes if I was actually struggling in the class that I thought had been my best. I went straight to the tower building where most of the teachers had their offices to see how I was really doing. I talked to each teacher one by one, and what I found was that I was struggling in most of my classes. I walked into the tower building hoping I was doing all right, but I left totally stressed. I needed to make up work in every class, and I only had three weeks to get it in.

I went straight to the lab and started to write the papers I didn't turn in. At the end of the semester, I turned in all the late work, and in most of my classes, I earned B's. I ended with all A's on my last couple of quizzes and my final in math class, and I earned an A for my overall grade. Still, I didn't feel good about the grades because I knew I really didn't deserve to pass. It wasn't because I didn't do the work that I felt that way but because I had not put forth my best effort. After a long hard look at my life and a truthful examination of my choices, I realized that if I were to make my dream of helping African American youth come true, I would have to give up something.

I made the decision to put aside anything that did not move me closer to the fulfillment of my goal to help African American youths. My dad always used to tell me: "Only the man who finds his focus will find success and happiness in life." I found my focus in education and went after my dreams with all my heart. I stopped going to parties, barbecues, and hanging out with women and friends unless they were from school. I won't say it was easy or that it wasn't lonely and boring at times, but no one else in my life wanted what I did, so I had to move past them. I found comfort in those times that I was lonely by meditating and searching my soul for the corruption that still lingered within me. Through introspection, I learned how to be honest about who I was and gained the strength and understanding to change.

Once I learned how to be understanding, I realized that most of the people I knew were manipulating me. In those days, I was a very giving man, and I loved to help others, but most people took advantage of this fact and used it for their benefit. I remember in 2012, I reconnected with an old friend named Billy. Billy and I were friends when we were young. He was a few years younger than me, so sometimes I would walk him home when we were kids.

We also ran in the same neighborhood as young adults, but when I lost my mind, he avoided me and didn't help me when he saw me sitting in the neighborhood. Nevertheless, life has a way of bringing you face to face with the people you have hurt or disrespected while you were doing well when you are at your most vulnerable. When I met Billy on the streets of Oakland, he was just out of jail, broke, and living with his girlfriend's family.

As I was rolling down Broadway in downtown Oakland, someone stepped in front of my chair. I looked up as I heard a man's voice say, "What's up, Gz?"

I said, "Billy? What's up? How you been, and where you going?"

"I was trying to sell this Bluetooth. It's the top of the line."

"Man, what's up? Why you out here like this? How much you trying to get, and why?"

"I need $70 dollars to pay the rent in the hotel me and my girl and her son is at," He said. "We were staying at her mom's house, but we had to leave. So, we been at that hotel for three weeks. We have an agency that's gonna help us pay rent, but we have to find a place."

Without any more questions, I reached into my pocket, pulled out a $100 bill, and handed it to him. He didn't see it coming and was so surprised that he just stopped and looked very deeply at me. "Man, I can't take this."

I said, "Man, stop playing. You need it, I have it, and I love you, so take it because I'm doing good. It won't hurt me."

He reached out his hand and took it but insisted that I take the Bluetooth.

He then asked, "What you up to these days, Gz? And how did you come back? Last time I saw you, you were sitting at a bus stop on Market talking to yourself and picking cigarette butts up off the ground."

"Man, it was God," I answered. "He brought me out and transformed my life. I'm studying at Laney College trying to earn two degrees—one in social science and the other in history. I'm good there, and check this out: I have a 3.55 GPA. Can you believe it?"

He said, "Yeah, I can believe it, Gz, because you were always smarter than us. I saw that in you even back then. It was something different about you. It was like you picked up things quicker than we did, but you were just small and quiet."

I said, "Thanks." However, I held his words within my heart and often pondered them over the time we spent together.

Billy moved into my house a couple of months later, and although he said he wouldn't use or disrespect me as he saw others do, in the end he did exactly that. Billy was still using drugs and carrying guns. I understood, but I told him he couldn't bring that stuff to my house. I also asked that he not come to my house high—this meant no powder cocaine, weed, or alcohol. But every time he came, he was on something, sometimes on all three. While making a mess and seeing there was stuff to be done in the house, he never offered to help or clean it. As an experiment, I left the house dirty just to see how long he would walk over things on the floor that should have been picked up. I was very patient with him and never complained or asked him to do anything, but I just watched to see what he would do or how far he would push it. Billy stayed with me for about a month, and the whole time I said nothing about his behavior. But the opportunity presented itself a few weeks later.

Billy came by one day just to talk, and I listened. He said, "Gz, I see how your kids and family treat you, and when I came to stay with you I didn't want to be like them."

I said, "But that's what you did."

He bowed his head. "How?"

I said, "You stayed here for three or four weeks, but ask yourself how many times you offered to clean up or take out the garbage? Plus, I asked you not to come here high, but each time you came, you admitted you were on something; and you even brought alcohol into my house and put it in my refrigerator. So, ask yourself how did you treat me?"

He said, "Man Gz, I'm sorry. I didn't realize, but I never asked or tried to clean up because I felt like you wouldn't want me to. You know some people would look down on me if I started to clean up their house, because I feel like they would think I was acting like it was my house."

"If you really thought that way, why do you think I let you stay here for all those days?" I asked. "I watched as you actually made yourself at home. You went in the kitchen and made something to eat when you wanted to, and you came in when you wanted to. You even brought whatever you wanted to in the house, so why did you think it was all right to not clean up?"

That night I realized just how much I had grown, never showing any emotion as I talked to Billy. Yes, I told him that he had disrespected me and my house, but I felt nothing because of it. I merely told him what I saw and thought as he lived in my house. I wasn't trying to make him feel some kind of way, nor did I need an apology. I just wanted him to realize what he had done. I really understood why he didn't do anything and why he felt it was all right to do the things he had done while he lived in my house. It wasn't that he actually was trying to disrespect me, but he never thought how his actions would affect me. He was what I had once been, but the only difference was that I had grown. When I was in the streets, I had done worse to people, like smoking in Tunisia's house even though I knew she would come home with her baby. I guess it was these thoughts that helped me understand, and through understanding I gained sympathy. I really felt sorry for him because he really didn't know what life was truly about. It's not just what you want to do, or what makes you happy. It's knowing how what I want to do affects others and having the desire to do only what builds others up or helps another. That's where true happiness springs from. Billy left my house that day and never returned. Whether it was because he felt guilty or because he had other things that he felt were more important I can't say. But he was gone all the same.

The Struggle and the Focus

By the beginning of 2013, my best friend Randy was released from jail and was living in a nursing home in East Oakland. School was getting very challenging, but I made time to see him and have Bible studies with him. Randy was older than me, but he often called me his big brother. I guessed it was because of the way I helped him. Randy and I were as thick as thieves—he helped me and I helped him. In life you would be lucky to find two or three people who would treat you as you treat them. Randy was just that sort of person, because he never denied me anything. While I was on drugs, he told me that he wouldn't fix me every day because he didn't want me to depend on him. I never held that against him because I knew he did this out of love. By the time he was released, his health was deteriorating.

Randy had always had problems breathing because of his past drug use. His lungs were so bad that the doctors told him they wouldn't be able to sustain him. After his release from jail, he started to have more complications with his breathing and was hospitalized more often. He would often slip into a coma, and once he awoke he would need to be placed on a breathing machine. The doctors told us that if he wanted to live, he would need to stay on the machine. Even though I tried to counsel him that it was for the best, he often fought against it. I remember one conversation that we had concerning the breathing machine.

"Randy, if you want to live, stay on the machine," I told him.

After some thought he replied, "Fred, I know you care and want the best for me, but I'm not gon' be on that machine. The doctors can't say what will happen to me because I believe that God has the last word. I can't just lie in that bed. That to me is worse than dying. I need to be in life, and although you love me and I know you want the best, I'm trusting that God will help me."

What could I have said against that? I had taught him each week about the love of God, His will and His strength, and now he wanted to place his life in God's hands. I just said, "You're right, Randy: if it's His will for you to live, you will live and nothing will stop it."

After that conversation, we never discussed it again, and as he believed, Randy didn't just die but lived three years longer after he was released from jail. Randy fought to live, but in the end, he could not overcome the problems that came out of his youth. In the last three years of his life, he was in the hospital or nursing home more than he was at home. I followed him all over the Bay area, from one nursing home to another. When he slipped into a coma—which he often did in the end—I was right there when he awoke, and he appreciated it. When he went to the hospital that last time, I was one day too late—he died the day before I went to see him. Randy died while I was in the middle of a semester at Laney College; although I still went to class, my heart was not in it.

The loss of Randy hit me very hard. I had lost many friends in my youth, but none of them were as close to me as Randy. I missed my friend and had no one close enough to me to take his place, so I grieved for a long time. All the while, my grades suffered. I could not focus, and every class was torture to sit through. All I wanted to do was sit at the lake and remember our times together—until I had a talk with his sister, Jane. One day while I was sitting at Lake Merritt thinking and listening to music, Jane called me.

I picked up the phone. "Hello?"

"Hello, Fred. It's Jane, Randy's sister. How are you holding up?"

"I'm all right, but I really miss Randy. I can't focus in class, and my grades are falling."

She said, "I understand, but you have to get back on the horse because that's what Randy would've wanted. I miss him too. You know, I have his ashes on my mantel, and sometimes I just sit and stare at them and think of him.

"You know he used to talk about you all the time because he was so proud of you. It was as if he lived his dream of going to school through you. So much so that my mother called me one day and asked, 'Who is this Fred guy?' I saw a real change in my brother after you guys started to hang out. He had always been in trouble, but I saw him wanting to be closer to God in the end, and I really think that was because of you. He told me how you would go and do Bible studies with him. He really enjoyed that."

That surprised me. "At the time, I couldn't tell because he would always fall asleep right in the middle of it," I told her. We both laughed. "Yeah, that was Randy."

"Fred, do it for him," Jane encouraged me. "I believe he's looking down on us, so don't let him down." Just as she said that, someone in her house called her, so she said, "I have to go, but think about what I said, all right? Bye."

By reminding me of how proud Randy was of me for going back to school, Jane reignited the fire I had for learning. When that conversation was done, I had found my focus again. I told myself that I would dedicate my rise in education to him: each A I received, we would earn together. Every stage I accomplished would be for him, and whatever I would become or do in life, we would become or do together. I started that next semester with a love in my heart, a love for not just Randy but for mental growth and a greater love and appreciation of life.

When the semester started, I hit the ground running and dove head first into my studies. At the beginning of every class, the teacher gave out a syllabus indicating the assignments from the start of the class until we completed the course. I was so focused that I would quickly knock out each week's assignment, and sometimes I was two or three weeks ahead of the class. By the end of my classes, I would just be attending because I had already completed all the work two weeks ahead of time. While many teachers fertilized the seeds of my understanding during this semester until it grew into a mighty oak, none were so endearing to me than Ms. E. Ms. E was a fair-skinned Greek woman of about thirty-three who stood about 5'6". She had long flowing black hair and a beautiful, outgoing personality. Unlike most teachers, Ms. E was always willing to share her joys and struggles with her classes.

For this, she was not just loved for her teaching, which was excellent, but because to us she was a friend. Ms. E took a liking to me, and we began a friendship that has lasted to this day. Without the motivating and encouraging spirits of Ms. Fuller and Ms. E, this book would have just stayed a dream. However, she took a personal interest in my success and was never too busy to offer a kind word, proofreading for my book, or just casual conversation. I saw myself through her eyes: I didn't believe in myself, but because she believed in me, I thrived. That next year I received A's and B's for my fall, spring, and summer classes and earned a spot on the dean's list. I completed my educational requirements in the summer of 2014, and in the process, I earned two Associate in Arts degrees—one in Social Science, and the other in African American History—while maintaining a 3.5 GPA. After completing the curriculum for Laney, I decided to go further and continue my education at Holy Names University.

Chapter 10

The Beginning of Understanding

A dream is like water; it can either sustain, perpetuate, or destroy depending on how it is applied or not applied to a person's life. My dreams of helping African American youths in my community nourished my motivation and kept the fires of progress burning within my heart. My dreams also helped me maintain focus, and as small streams feed the great ocean, my accomplishment of the little goals led to a flowing within my mind, which fed the bigger dreams. As I stood at the precipice of life, higher education, and growth, I remembered an experience of my youth.

When I was fourteen years old, a friend and I used to go hang out with some girls on the campus of San Francisco State University. One day as we were walking and horse-playing, I suddenly noticed the people around us. There were Asians, Whites, and African American young people not much older than we were walking all around us. I realized that although we were all walking, they had a different sort of walk—they looked like they were going somewhere or had a purpose. For a split second, I desperately wanted to follow them. I wanted for myself what I saw in them, even though I didn't understand what that was. Although I didn't realize it at the time, it wasn't their current destinations but their future destinations in life that I wanted for myself. As I entered into the stream of the crowd that walks with intention, purpose, and diligence, I thought back to that moment. I realized that my God heard me, and now I am allowing Him to finally do for me what I could never do for myself—change me. However, I also understood that for me to really achieve my dreams, I first needed to overcome my insecurities, fears, and flesh.

I have often been told that life is like a class that is always in session, but only those who can glean the lessons from their surroundings pass from one stage to the other. So, I started to analyze everything: people, situations I encountered, books, words, my thoughts, my fears, and my feelings—and slowly, I learned introspection. Day-by-day, and class-by-class, the things I learned at Holy Names University and my desire to serve God helped me understand the true meaning of the old saying: "It's not what people do to you but how you respond to what they do that matters." Through self-examination I slowly learned that because of my past, I had developed feelings that automatically responded to certain situations without conscious thought. This revelation forced me to see myself in a different light. I realized that I was self-centered, that I only felt certain ways in situations because I only thought of how it related to and affected me.

I realized that what I lacked was understanding, empathy, and compassion for others. With that in mind, I prayed and sought the way to be able to understand how others felt. I put my desires, my anger, and my ego to the side and started to see from a broader perspective. In every situation I encountered after that, when I felt negative emotions, before I chose to blame others for it, I started to ask myself, *"Why? Why do I feel anger because of what someone said? Why do I feel sad because of what someone did or didn't do?"* By asking these and other introspective questions, I forced myself to look within for my answers and the causes of my emotions. By doing this, I slowly began to stop blaming others for my feeling certain emotions that really had more to do with my shortcomings than with theirs. I must say without God I don't believe I would have seen myself truthfully. I would have continued to believe the lies that kept me impulsive, blind, and ignorant of my true problems.

Through introspection I gained understanding not just of myself, but I also learned to see the lack of self-examination in others. I was able to understand when others were mad, or felt I disrespected them, or were sad because of me. I recognized that in some situations, the real problem was with them. I learned not to respond with anger, frustration, or defensiveness but to pity them and to ask questions that would bring out the real problems.

While I attended Holy Names University, there were many people and situations that challenged me. They helped me gain a fuller knowledge of myself as well as the skills to deal with other people who had never asked the questions I was constantly wrestling with.

I started Holy Names in the fall of 2014. My first day there, I met two women who were also there to study psychology. Their names were Kate and Joan.

Kate was a sixty-seven-year-old woman who lived by the lake. She drove to school, and since both she and Joan lived close to each other, Joan always caught a ride with her to school. These two women were both African American, but they were as different as night and day. Kate was a very reserved and thoughtful person, but Joan was a very outspoken and "ghetto" older lady of about fifty-one. Kate was rather thick with a dark caramel complexion and long blackish-grey hair. The shape of her head and her complexion made her resemble an Ethiopian woman. Joan wore her hair short, was rather dark-skinned, and was very skinny, but she always had a big smile no matter the situation.

More important than their physical differences was the contrast of their characters. While we were all friends, I was closer to Kate, but I never neglected Joan. This was because Kate was very independent and self-willed. She needed me for nothing except maybe an idea or two for a paper. Joan, on the other hand, was once a drug addict, and because of this, she was one who always tried to use people. She was always asking for a ride, cigarettes, a few dollars, or for me to do her papers, but she never paid us back or was willing to help others. Kate was the complete opposite: she was a giver, helper, and very compassionate. Their friendship was volatile and doomed from the start.

One day an upset Kate called me. Hearing the anger in her voice, I already knew it was because of Joan. "Fred, Joan is scan'less! She's been riding with me this whole time and has never given me any money for gas."

"Did y'all have an agreement?" I asked, "Because you should have already known she wasn't going to give up any money."

"Yeah, she kept saying she would give me some money when she got her school money."

I said, "Come on now, you knew she wasn't giving you nothing. That's just who she is; she's not going to give no one her money. For her, money is hard to come by, so she desperately holds on to it. She probably really wanted to, but once she realized that it would take from her pot, she thought better."

Kate wasn't sympathetic. "I'm not like that. If I say something to someone or make a promise, I live up to it. She ain't gon' get nowhere doing stuff like that."

"Kate, do you need the money?" I asked.

"No, but that's not the point. For me it's about the principle. She rode with me all that time, so she should do what she said she was going to do. She straight clowned (embarrassed) me. After we got our money, I waited for three weeks, and then I called her and asked about the money. You know she had the nerve to get mad and tell me don't be asking her about her money."

I silently laughed to myself; I couldn't understand why Kate didn't see all this coming. We were around Joan for two semesters, and I thought we all could see her character clearly. The way Joan was always nickel-and-diming us for her beer money but never paying any of us back, I could have told Kate she was lying. Plus, when Kate said she really didn't need the money, I really couldn't understand what the problem was.

"Kate, if you don't need the money and you know where she comes from, why don't you just forgive her and move on?" I asked. "Why does it bother you so much, and why don't you give her a break and have some understanding? She's not doing something to you that she wouldn't do to others. That's just who she is and what she does. So please don't take it personally. Why don't you try to see it from her point of view? I'm not saying she's right, but I just want you to see why it's right for her. She doesn't get a lot of money and probably never had a lot of money in her life because of her habits. So now she's getting $3000 all at once, but that might be the most she has ever had at one time."

Kate answered, "I don't care about all that. She shouldn't have gotten in my car if she didn't want to help with gas, because she knows the car needs gas."

I didn't respond. I just thought to myself, "Without understanding, one makes other people's problems theirs." As I meditated on the conversation, I saw clearly how Joan's character defects spilled over onto Kate. Although Kate spent a lot of time with Joan, she had never gotten to know Joan. She never looked beyond their casual conversations and the pleasant platitudes to Joan's true self. Because of that, she couldn't show Joan compassion, understanding, or forgiveness. In the end Joan, being true to herself, moved on after they had parted ways, but Kate was stuck. Joan's defects made her bitter. Kate didn't forgive, and in all actuality, she couldn't forgive.

As I have come to realize, forgiveness can be likened to how humans breathe. We do it every second of the day and with great ease, but without oxygen, breathing would be impossible. We need the one to do the other, and as our breathing depends on something we cannot see; so forgiveness is dependent not on what we see but what we consciously know of others. By taking all that makes a person—history, character, desires, strengths, weaknesses, and intentions—into account, we can understand why people do what they do. Here was where one of my greatest lessons in understanding, judgement, and forgiveness was formed: n*ever judge a situation or a person's actions without first understanding the situation or the person, and never allow a negative situation or a person's actions or defects stop your growth.* Thus, school became so much more than a formal education. It became an understanding of truth, an education in who I really was and wanted to be, and a lesson in humility, change, and growth.

Although I was changing, there was no one in my circle who matched my growth or desire for change. I was like the freed man of the Plato allegory. In his allegory, Plato describes a family that had been chained to the ground in a cave all their lives. While lying chained, they could only hear mumbled voices and see shadows on the walls around them. However, one man started to fumble with his chains, and after some struggling, he broke them and freed himself. As he stood up and looked around, he could see a fire that burned behind them, and as he walked around he saw the opening to the cave and ventured outside.

Standing at the precipice, he looked at the world outside of the cave, a world he had never seen nor could he have ever imagined. And instead of climbing down, he went back into the cave to tell his family and friends. Although he could clearly capture the wonders he saw with words and gestures, he could not convince them it was true. Plato says that they resisted his words so forcefully that if they could have, they would have killed him. I had seen the real world and eagerly desired to go and tell my family and friends, but no one could believe that it was better than what they had known all their lives. Thus, I became an outcast, and in all my relationships, my intentions and actions were misunderstood or ridiculed. School was an escape from this. It not only brought enlightenment; it also brought with it a focus, a direction, and a place where I belonged.

A Look Back to Move Forward

As I pursued my BA in psychology, every class led me to the idea for a new goal. Like a tree, I started as a sapling, but as I grew my branches sprouted out—and on each branch sprouted multiple stems that brought forth beautifully colored leaves.

I started multiple projects. I remember one day as I was rolling down a hallway during the summer session in 2015, I noticed a sign asking students to enroll in a creative writing class for the fall semester. It caught my attention because it was a nonfiction writing class. The sign asked students to bring their sports stories, their memoirs, and their vacation tales. I thought of Ms. Fuller and Ms. E and how they always told me that I should write a book, so I signed up.

On the break leading up to the fall semester, I decided to take time out to start my book. I determined to sit down and write thirty pages for the class. At the start of my book, the experiences came back to me easily. After about ten pages I was really into it, so I spent most of my time writing. The best part was writing the conversations I had with the people of my past. As I wrote, I could clearly picture them and capture how each personality said this or that, and by the time fall semester rolled around, I had accumulated forty pages of my story. I was eager to start the class and see what people thought of not only the story, but also of my writing. But I became very discouraged after the first class because the teacher, Ms. Ralker, gave me a twelve-page limit. I thought about how to reduce forty pages into twelve and still capture the progression of my life.

Finally, I asked, "Ms. Ralker, can I do the page count usually reserved for the grad students (which was twenty pages)?"

She said, "Frederick, that number was given for a reason, so please just do twelve pages."

I grumbled and complained to each person I encountered after that, until I ran into a doctor at the clinic I went to. As I was complaining to her, she stopped me. "What is the problem with what the teacher is asking you to do?"

"I have forty well-thought-out pages. Each paragraph connects to the next, and I believe all of it is important."

She nodded. "Yes, it may all be important, but how much of it is necessary to make the point about or to show the meaning of each experience? I advise you to get rid of the window dressing and get to the point quick. I'm sure it will boil down to close to twelve pages."

I said, "I understand and I'll try that," but inside I quickly dismissed her advice; I wanted to complain, not find a solution.

Though I didn't think much of what she said at the time, once in front of my paper, I quickly saw the window dressing clearly. I started to cut parts out until by the end of the class, I had sixteen solid pages. The last day of the class I was so proud of the work I had done and couldn't wait to get feedback from the teacher and my classmates. Part of the requirement of the class was that we had to exchange papers with a classmate. I chose a white young lady named Jackie who was always helpful and open with me during the time we spent in class. After a ten-minute break for us to read each other's papers, the teacher asked, "Who would like to go first?"

Since this was my first creative writing class, I waited to see what the others had to say about each other's papers so I would know what she was looking for. A Hawaiian young man named Jay raised his hand and started to critique the sports story of a young white kid named Billy. Billy wrote his story about a young basketball player's struggles to be a single dad, student, and athlete. That caught my attention, and I was very interested in what Jay had to say. From the time we spent in class doing writing exercises, I believed Jay was a phenomenal writer.

As Jay started to speak, the whole class sat on the edges of their seats wondering what he was going to say. He began, "I first want to say this is a well written paper, and the story was very interesting. But I do think it could be better if you spoke more to the child in the story, to see how he felt during the times his father was in class and at basketball practice. Although you spent a lot of time talking to Tony's teammates, I would have liked to see more of his struggles, such as how much time he spent on the road, in class, and at practice, versus how much time he actually spent with his son and how he justified it to himself. I think this would have shown what I believe you actually wanted to accomplish with this story."

I was at a loss. I thought his critique was actually saying that Billy didn't accomplish what he set out to do with his story. One of the most important rules of peer review was not to write another person's paper but to critique what he or she had done. In my opinion, he did just that and tried to tell Billy what his story should be instead of examining what it actually was, and the teacher said nothing. I glanced over at Jackie, who was still reading and marking on my paper, and silently second-guessed my story. As she raised her hand to be next to speak, a small chill ran up my spine.

A wise woman once told me, "No matter how many marks are on the page or what someone has to say about your paper, if you believe that it's done, then it's done. Your paper is a gateway into your mind, and if it speaks a certain way and you're willing to accept the grade, keep it. A critique is just someone else's ideas of what should be. However, in many instances, they have no clue about who you are, and all they see are the words, not the emotions that went into it."

As I sat there, I closed my eyes and said to myself, "It's me and I'm beautiful, so what I wrote is beautiful." I opened my eyes as Jackie started to speak.

She started, "Frederick, I want to say this was a really good story. I was on the edge of my seat the whole way through. Your realizations of where your struggles started in terms of your adopting the different values and morals was very interesting. It made me look back into my life to see how I was formed. But one thing I would like to see more of is the environment being brought to life. Also, I would like to know more about your family and what you termed 'the struggle to live.' But overall, except for that and a few grammatical mistakes, it was very good writing and riveting. You're on to something here, and I encourage you to just keep writing."

I silently thanked God for the struggle, for the pain, for the change, and growth—and asked Him that if it was his will that I start the book now, then let it be done. I learned a valuable lesson in this situation, which I now live by: *Never judge a person by their skin color or upbringing, but judge them by their character and actions because they just might surprise you.*

That semester more than any other helped my confidence and self-esteem when it came to my writing. I continued to write as Jackie had advised me to. The book took on a life of its own. I made sure that my grades didn't suffer, and the book became my passion. I lived for the breaks, and I tried to always stay two weeks ahead of my work so I could use the time to write the book. Due to my newfound belief in my writing ability, I took greater care with my school papers. I sought help from tutors, friends, and teachers to help me improve. One special young lady who was never too busy to help me was a young Asian lady named July.

The Friendship and the Awakening

While there were some people just like my family who misunderstood me, there were also some who were growing as I was. The teachers at school were a source of comfort for me, but my classmates provided friendship as well. In my second year at Holy Names, I met a very intelligent Asian young lady named July. July was not the stereotypical Asian woman. She was about thirty-four years old, stood about 5'6", and had a thick frame covered with different brightly colored tattoos. She was also very outgoing. The one thing I noticed first about July was her big smile. When she laughed, her eyes appeared to close and her chubby cheeks lifted, which produced a beautiful and very inviting smile. In a class, where most were mentally asleep or eagerly awaiting its end, July and I stood out like sore thumbs. We were both studying psychology, but we chose to apply it in different ways. July liked the administrative side, whereas I decided to choose counseling. Although July was Asian, we hit it off through our shared understanding of the world. We had overcome similar challenges in our lives. She had also been addicted to drugs, lived in the Tenderloin, and understood how people succumbed to crime because of their need to survive.

July was one of the smartest students I met while at the school. She had a very challenging job and sometimes took four or five classes as well. When there was something I needed help with in a class, I went to her, and she was always happy to lend a hand. Her last semester at Holy Names, we had a very challenging senior class together where the young adults unconsciously segregated themselves from July and me. Most of the students sat to the left side of the class, and July and I sat in the front and far to the right. We were alright with it and only noticed when it was time to get into groups and there was only us in our group.

July said, "I guess it's our age." Then we both chuckled to ourselves.

We developed a twenty-page research paper with a presentation at the end of the class. I decided to tackle the topic of the emotional, physical, and psychological effects of perceived racism. Although I completed the task, I had no idea how to make a presentation board, so I went to July for help.

"July, can you help me?" I asked. "I'm lost with how to do my board. I'm not very good at cutting and pasting stuff."

July said, "If you have the money you can get it printed."

"Printed? How much does that cost? And where do I go for that?"

"I know a place and it's easy," She assured me. "All you do is use PowerPoint in Word. You put the dimensions you want your board to be, put it the way you want it, and they'll print it out on a thick paper. Then all you do is paste the printed paper on the presentation board, and it's done. And it's cheap: it only costs about $89 dollars at the place I go to for work. When you go there, just tell them you know me and they'll give you a discount."

"I'm doing that. Just give me the name of the place. Also, can you show me how to do it in PowerPoint?" I asked.

July nodded. "Sure, just take out your computer and we can do it now."

We sat in the lounge for about an hour and half and put together an outline for my board.

I took pride in the research I had done in the class. I thought it was a meaningful topic. I decided on the topic of racism because I wanted to see just how much racism affected the African American community. What I found was very shocking to me. I learned that when people perceive that they are being discriminated against because of their race, it affects their bodies and their minds. Racism affects a person's emotional, psychological, and physical functions. It can even lead to diseases that could end in death. The information I found in the psychological journals forced me to ask the question: "If racism is deleterious to the health of people who perceive it in their lives, why is it that the government has not created or enforced laws for the equality of all people?" My answer to that question produced a value that I have carried with me since that day: *"I am my brother's keeper. If the human race is to be elevated, it's up to me to be a part of the solution and a source of light to help those who still live in the night."* I could not wait until the last class to present my findings to the faculty, visitors, and students who would attend the meeting.

The day of the presentations brought with it a sense of anxiety as well as excitement. My greatest fear was that when they called my name there would be no family in the audience to support me and my hard work. The psychological presentations were to be held in a building that was accessible for me, and parking was provided for our families and friends. The building was small, so if none of my family showed up, their absence would be witnessed by all that attended, and I just couldn't bear that. I started to worry, but leading up to the presentation day, I mentioned it to my daughter, and she quickly gave me her response.

"Yeah, Tootie, I would love to come see what you did in the class. Just let me know when it is and what time to be there."

"Thank you, Anita," I said, relieved. "I was really worried no one would show up."

"Even though sometimes we don't show it, or it seems like we don't care about what you're doing, we all are very proud of you for going back to school. It's just that we have our lives that take up most of our time, but we recognize all your hard work," Anita explained. "I mean, we know how you wake up at the crack of dawn and be at the coffee shop doing work before most of us wake up. We see your determination, and even if we don't show it, we all know you are trying to set an example for us and we love you for it."

I just smiled, feeling grateful that they actually understood. "Thank you, Anita. That means a lot. And I know one day each of y'all in y'all own time will follow in my footsteps in education."

Anita gave me a shy smile. "I believe that, too. It's just now we having too much fun, but when we are ready to settle down, we all know where to go, and that's because of you."

That conversation had the exact words I needed to hear at that moment because all I was attempting to accomplish was for them. Not only was I desperately trying to set an example and gain the tools to be a source of help in the future, I also wanted to leave them with something that could sustain them even as adults once I was gone. Their understanding of my motivations solidified my determination and helped me to gain the strength to continue the course unshaken by the whirlwind of weariness and mental exhaustion.

From that conversation, I gained an understanding of words and gained a value that, if I remembered, would help me in my chosen profession: The words a person speaks may be simple and emotionless to them, but to the hearer of those words, they will either be a source to build the spiritual, mental, and emotional state or a destructive power to tear down one or all three. Therefore, always think before you speak, and consider the fears and spiritual, mental, and emotional states of others first.

Armed with Anita's words and a very detailed presentation, I began my journey to the college. As I entered the building, I noticed that it was filled with the friends and family of the students. Through the crowd, I recognized July's familiar face, and when our eyes met, she motioned for me to come closer. July, ever so helpful and friendly, had saved me a space next to her poster.

Her first words to me were, "Frederick, your poster looks great!"

I turned to look at her poster and gave her a big Kool-Aid smile. "Yours is better, but I knew you were going to knock it out of the park."

She smiled back. "Oh, Frederick, stop it—we both did a great job." Then she lightly touched my shoulder and walked off.

The teachers allowed the class and the visitors time to walk around the hall and check out the posters that were being presented. No poster was overlooked, but each member of the class and every visitor stopped at each one and asked questions about the research. Then about fifteen minutes after we arrived, the meeting was called to order, and Ms. Isaac took the podium. As she started to speak, she let out a big sigh and thanked the class for all of the hard work we put into completing the research projects.

She said, "Everyone knows that my class is one of the most challenging, but each of the students put their all into the research, and the posters that are presented here today prove as much. The psychology program here at Holy Names tries to prepare our students to think independently, critically, and deeply about the world, its people, and each human situation that we encounter as people. Therefore, when you are talking to one of the students at home and you start to wonder if they're analyzing you, I can honestly say, yeah, they are." As she said this, the whole hall started to laugh, with the students leaning over to each other and saying, "My family always ask me that."

After the hall settled down, Ms. Isaac continued, "Look around the hall and you will see research on topics from racism to child development, and please, once I've finished announcing the class, walk around and check out each poster."

Although I was excited to present my research and could not wait to answer the questions of the visitors, I was quickly disappointed because she took two hours to announce the students. By the time she was done, my butt was hurting, and all I wanted to do was go home and lie down. It was so long that once our introductions were completed, most of the students were trying to find a way to leave without being seen by the teachers. Slowly, one by one, we all slipped away, and as I walked to the car with one of the students named Tai, we talked about how glad we were that it was finally over.

Tai asked me, "Frederick, how many more senior classes do you have left?"

I"I just have field methods to go and two general education classes, and I'm done. Thank God for that."

"It's almost over. Just a little more to go, so we have to push through. But you'll like Sireo's class, because all you have to do is listen to his comments and you'll get an A." As she was climbing into her car, she added, "His class is one of the easier senior classes we have to take, so you'll be fine, I'm sure."

I rolled off feeling confident that I could make it through field methods with no trouble and looking forward to my break.

Chapter 11

Pursuit of Freedom

At the start of the 2016, I set some goals that would lead me to get back to driving again. I eagerly anticipated the summer break, as I had saved up enough money to buy a car. The other goals I set were getting a push wheelchair, finding money to buy hand controls, and finding money to put them on a car. By the summer, I had accomplished three of my four goals; all I needed to do was find money to put the controls on the car I had bought. I started by petitioning the California Department of Rehabilitation for the money to install the controls. Although they had agreed to it before I started taking driving lessons, in the end they rescinded the decision and left me waiting. I was upset, but there was nothing I could do, so I complained to my family and friends.

One of my closest friends at the time was an older African American man named Edward. Edward was what we called an O.G. because he had been in the street life, but unlike other older men, he had actually learned a lot and gained wisdom because of his experiences. Edward was caramel-complexioned, stood 6'3", and had straight hair. He was a hard man, and he had no problem speaking his mind or telling others what he really thought of them. He was a straightforward man, but he also had a heart of gold and was always looking for ways to help those in need. For some reason, he took a liking to me, and he was always there to lend a helping hand when I needed one. As we were talking, I mentioned that the Department of Rehab wasn't helping me with the car, and Edward stopped me.

"Frederick, you don't need them people to help you. Stop letting others dictate to you what you can and can't have. If you want the controls on the car, you can do it yourself. You have a partner over here that is always willing to help you. You're a good dude, and you doing good things in life, so I would love to help you on your way. How about this? I'll pay half of the cost up to $1,500, and that way you won't need no one."

I was taken totally off-guard because I wasn't expecting that, but I was grateful. So, I said, "Thank you, Edward."

Edward, being the humble man that he is, chuckled and said, "Don't do that. You don't have to say thank you. It's already said by the way you are and how you treat me; this is just what partners do for each other. For me it's nothing special. You're doing good things, so good things come to you. Don't thank me. Thank God, Fred, for giving me the heart to do it for you."

I started to call around to check how much it would be to buy hand controls and to have them installed. What I found was that most of the companies that did the installation charged anywhere from $2,000 to

$3,500. There was no way I was going to allow Edward to pay half of that much. Although I know he would not have cared, I wanted to think of him like he was thinking of me. Then out of the blue, another friend of mine offered to give me a pair of hand controls for free. Her named was Annette, and she was also in a wheelchair and had just gone through the process of getting her driver's license. Annette was a young Latina of about twenty-five. She was one of the most beautiful women I met while at Laney College: she never complained, but she had a thousand reasons why she could have.

Annette was born with a learning disability and spinal problems, but she was one of the happiest people I've met. She did not let her challenges stop her or become a source of depression. She was fair-skinned, short, very skinny, and had long flowing dark hair that she often colored. Although she had many problems, she was very independent and never allowed others to push her in her chair. She struggled through school but awoke each day to carry on. Her spirit was so inviting that all who knew her could not help but like her. When she entered a room, it was like she brought with her the noonday sun, because she lit up the room with her beautiful personality. When she offered to just give me the hand controls, I was not surprised, because that was just the kind of person she was.

Annette's contribution to the fulfillment of my goal moved up my expected driving date. I had planned to be on the road by February of 2017, but it was looking like I would have everything I needed by December of 2016. I began to take driving lessons—not because I didn't know how to drive but because I lacked confidence behind the wheel. I went out on the road six times, and it was like I had never stopped driving because everything just came back as I drove. I wanted to keep up my lessons for the whole month of December until after my sixth lesson when I mentioned my plans to the instructor.

"Tina, let's make four more appointments to the end of December, and after they're completed, I'll sign up to take the driving test, alright?"

Tina smiled and placed her hand on my shoulder. "From what I've seen in these last few lessons, you're ready to take the test now, but I'll keep taking your money if you just want me to."

I smiled back. "Do you really think I'm ready? Because if so, I'll sign up today and call you with my appointment date. How much would it cost me to use your car to take the test? Because my car isn't fitted yet, plus it's kinda fast, and I'm not used to the car."

"It would be best to get the hand controls installed on your car," She replied. "That is the one you're going to be using all the time, but if you must use my car, it'll be $325."

"Alright, I'll call you after I make the appointment. Okay?"

As I was rolling away from her car, she yelled, "Frederick, I'll come get you an hour before the test, and we can get a little practice in. Also, if I don't see you again, it was my pleasure to meet you. Keep me posted to what's happening, alright?"

I went directly into the house and made an appointment to take the driving test at the El Cerrito DMV. I had three weeks until the test, and I was getting the controls on my car that next Monday. I thought the three weeks would give me time to practice with my car. That Monday, my daughter Anita and I were scheduled to take the car in to get fixed. Somehow, she got it in her head that until the car was modified, I would hand over the keys and send her into the streets by herself.

She came into the house and said, "Come on, hurry up. I got somewhere to be."

At that time, I was on the phone conducting personal business, so I motioned for her to wait. Once I was off the phone, I rolled into the living room and asked, "Nita, can you give me that chair, so I can transfer, and then we can go?"

She looked at me with daggers in her eyes. "What … you coming with us?"

"Yeah," I answered. "What, you thought I was just gon' give you the keys to my new car that I just paid ten thousand dollars for and haven't even drove yet? Anita, that's crazy, plus if she going what's the difference between us. If you really just going to turn in a paper, why can't I wait in the car, unless you had other plans you not telling me about?"

"Forget it, I'll just catch the bus," She said as she stormed pass me heading for the front door.

Her response hurt my heart because I very rarely said no to her about anything she asked of me. Children can be so selfish and self-centered that they completely overlook how their words and actions affect others. They just go about their day hurting and disrespecting the ones who love them the most. However, since I hate to have to beg someone to help me, I didn't even call her to see if she was still going to take me to put the controls on. Instead, I picked up my phone and started to make other plans.

I first called a friend who lived in my building, and as he picked up I said, "Hello, Larry, I need to ask a favor of you."

"What is it, Frederick? I'm always happy to help you."

"I need help getting my car to the shop to get the hand controls put on."

"What about Anita?" He asked. "I thought you said she was going to help you."

"She was supposed to, but she got mad at me for not letting her drive my car."

Larry sounded sympathetic. "Frederick, I feel for you. Everyone is always asking you for stuff, but when you need something, you have to ask a stranger. I mean no disrespect, Frederick, but you should really stop helping those who don't help you, because they just using you. But anyways, what day and time you want to go?"

"It's up to you, because I'm on your time."

"I can do it at 1:00 PM tomorrow," Larry assured me, but you have an account with Uber so we can get back home, right?"

I said, "Yeah, but not with Uber. I have one with Lyft."

But that night, my cousin Demetri called me and said that he could do it early the next morning. So, I chose to use him to help me get the car to the shop instead of Larry.

The next day, as we jumped into the car on our way to the shop to have the hand controls put on, the excitement I felt was overwhelming. All the way there, I kept saying to Demetri, "I'm 'bout to be driving."

He just looked over at me and smiled. "Yeah, Gz, you are."

When we arrived, the man came out in a wheelchair and took down the specs for what I wanted on the car. Then we began to talk about the rules to driving with the controls, and he revealed to me that there were some rules that did and didn't apply to me. As we talked, he said, "I'll take a look at your car and call you with a time to pick it up. I'll let you know how much it's going to cost then."

"Alright, but about what time tomorrow?" I asked.

"I'll call you about two or three."

I said, "Okay, but please give me a break on the price because I'm broke." After I said this, we all started to laugh, and then we walked off.

It seemed like the twenty-four hours I had to wait went by in no time. The mechanic called me at 1:00 PM and told me the car was ready to be picked up. But once I was told I could come get it, all the excitement left, and what replaced it was fear. It took me three hours to build up enough courage to go get it. I knew I had to get there by five o'clock because it was Friday and the shop was closed on the weekend. At three o'clock, I started to get ready to go get it, and by three-forty-five I was on my way.

When I arrived at the shop, I met the mechanic out front, and he said, "This is a nice car, and it's fast, so be careful."

"How much do I owe you?" I asked.

He said, "I gave you a break, so just give me five hundred and sixty dollars."

I dug into my pocket and handed him his money. I started to thank him profusely because I knew he didn't just give me a break but mercy—when I called around before I found his shop, everyone else wanted between two and three thousand dollars to do what he had just done for five hundred.

As we exchanged the keys for the money, it hit me that I was really going to have to drive the car home, and my anxiety rose. I turned and started to approach the car, all the while trying not to show him I was terrified because I didn't want him to regret putting the controls on the car. He turned and went back into the shop as I opened the door of the car.

The transfer into the car was easy, and the breakdown of the chair was as if I had been doing it all my life. But once I started the car, fear took over, and when I put it into drive and pulled down on the control, it sped off like a rocket. I immediately hit the brake then looked over at the door of the shop to see if anyone saw the mistake. Fortunately for me, they were all in the back, and no one could see me. It took me two hours of driving around the neighborhood around the shop to get used to the controls and the car's speed, but after three hours, I finally made it home.

Once home, I sat in the car and looked back over the steps I had taken to get to that point. I meditated on and had received the vision of being able to drive in February of 2016, and by December of that same year, that goal was accomplished. I realized that day by day I took some kind of step to help my dream become a reality. This revelation made me think that there are two dimensions that help people make their dreams come true: faith and discipline. And so a new value emerged: a dream is only as good as the faith one has in its accomplishment and the discipline one puts into working each day for its fulfillment.

A Welcome Distraction

By the time I received my driving license, the spring semester of 2017 was just about to begin. This semester I would take my last two classes, and I was eager to complete my Bachelor of Arts degree so I could attend graduate school. I didn't realize that although they were only intro classes into biology and sociology, this would be my toughest semester not because the classes were hard for me, but because I was mentally past them. Mentally, I was already in graduate school and taking classes. I couldn't find the time to actually do the work between driving, calling around to check on my graduate program, and taking care of the new women in my life— I was always behind. Though the work I did was always given very high marks, I just didn't want to do it. I could always find something better or more interesting to do than my work. It was like pulling teeth whenever I sat down to do the work. I was so out of it that during the semester I had gotten behind a week and didn't even know it. I turned in an assignment, and I really thought it was on time, but it was actually a week late. I had lost a week, and when I analyzed why, it was because of a new woman friend I had started to talk to.

Her name was Betty, and she was a beautiful flower that I truly believed God wanted me to water. She was a married woman who really loved her husband, but she was missing intimacy within her relationship. We connected but made it clear to each other that it would be a strictly platonic relationship. I met her at a local supermarket, and through her kindness, she made me feel welcomed. Betty was a very fair-skinned Puerto Rican woman who was about 52. She had a very beautiful smile that made the meanest of men smile back. She always had a pleasant word for all those who entered the store. When a person went into the store, he or she would not forget her because she just stood out. She wore a short hairstyle that had a light purple tint to it, and it made the beauty of her face stand out. As pretty as she was on the outside, it was no match for her inner beauty.

Betty had a very challenging life, but it did not dampen or corrupt the love within her. She was like me, a giver, and within all her relationships she was selfless. She cared for everyone no matter their position or economic status. She was a real wife and mother because she worked eight hours at a very challenging job, drove in traffic for two hours, took care of her grandkids, and she still found time to cook and clean each day. She had a humble and pleasant spirit that took me by surprise. It was through talking to her that I realized what I missed in a woman.

I found her warm spirit beautiful, and I loved her willingness to be patient and loving no matter the situation. Although we were only friends and never entertained any other thoughts or feelings about being together, she made me dissatisfied with my life. Not because anything had changed within it, but through her I remembered how wonderful being in love and having someone love me was. Many times while we talked and she spoke of her relationship, I wanted to experience those situations and feelings for myself. I remember one of our conversations about her interactions with her husband that had me daydreaming of my ex-wife.

"What are you doing?" I asked her.

She said, "Cleaning up."

"Does anyone ever help you or clean for you?"

Her response shocked me. "Sometimes when I'm washing dishes or cleaning, my husband dries the dishes, or we clean the house together."

Immediately I remembered my ex-wife and I because it wasn't the cleaning but the closeness we shared while cleaning I missed. We used to joke and laugh or talk about the family's problems, and it was those moments that brought us closer and joined our spirits together. It was the playful and funny parts of the relationship that talking to Betty brought to the forefront of my mind. Her conversations made me want more from life than just degrees, a career, and money. Now I had standards, and I wanted and needed someone that could measure up to them.

It wasn't that there weren't women who wanted to be in a relationship with me, there were women around me, but none were what I was looking for in a woman, so I kept them as friends. My most important standards were that she had to be understanding and patient. I believed that if these traits were within her, there would be no situation that we could not work through together. Most of the women I met had good things about them, but they had more things that I considered bad traits. There were some women who were users. They called when they needed something, but they never repaid what they borrowed. They felt that a true man was one who took care of his woman. However, I always asked: what do the woman do for the man? Most of these types of women thought by giving me sex they were paying their way, but I would say my sex is worth more than what they were giving. That comment always hit them where it hurts, and they would get mad. But I meant that, so they were quickly shuffled into the friend box. Then there were the women who held a man to a standard that they themselves were not living up to. There were so many women but so few who had actually worked on their characters.

In the end, after all the dating I had done, I only found friends, and that was alright with me. Through these women, I learned a valuable lesson: *one can have the love of a woman without actually making love to her because he who respects, encourages, motivates, listens to, genuinely cares for, and protects a woman's emotions will enter into a relationship that in some cases can be stronger than a marriage.*

From each of the women in my life, I gained something different. It wasn't sex I missed but intimacy. I truly believed that God would send that special woman when I was ready and able to maintain a household. While Betty made me crave a woman, deep down inside I knew I had more life to live before I would find the one sent by God. So I shared my life with the different women friends I had gained, and they were enough. I was able to get back to business and start taking my classes seriously.

Through Struggle Came Triumph

Although I had to play catch up, I was up to the task. I began to work on all my assignments as early as possible. My sociology class focused on race relations and racism, so I had no problem in that class, seeing that I had an A.A. degree in African American history. My biology class, however, was a totally different monster, and more so because I had not ever taken a bio class—I had to really study in order to pass the tests and do the homework. In the end, it came down to me getting thirty-five or higher out of fifty in order to pass.

The tests were not the difficult part, but trying to answer the questions to the teacher's expectations was the real problem. She was so rigid and particular that on one of my tests, I had put all the words in the right order and clearly showed how the body deals with high and low blood glucose, but I forgot to put an arrow tip at the end of the lines I used to connect the words, so she marked it wrong. She didn't even offer me partial credit for at least knowing the structure, direction, and pathways of insulin and positive and negative feedback. In the end, I barely passed, but that was all that I cared about.

With three weeks before graduation, I was informed that I was nominated to speak on behalf of the adult graduating class of 2017. I was shocked because this was an honor that I never saw coming. After I meditated on my experiences at the university, I realized that I had befriended, helped, or offered to help almost everyone in my cohort. There were few adult graduates who didn't know and like me in the psychology program. I began to see that it was a well-deserved honor and one that I silently wanted ever since my days at Laney College. As I meditated on just how far I'd come since the days on Oakdale and thought about all the life that was lived in between, I could only see God's mercy.

In that moment, I realized that I could be doing or could have become so many other things besides what I actually ended up doing and growing into. The things that stuck out in my mind were that I could have stayed in the streets like so many of my friends in the past, or my drug habit could've progressed until I was living on the streets and waking each day in search of my next hit. Those were a couple of the many paths that some of my old friends took. I could've stayed lost in my mind and walking the streets hearing voices and talking to myself, and the most fearful thought was that I could have been dead and never gotten the chance to change, see my children grow up, or have this opportunity. As I sat there, I started crying and felt so humbled by the love, mercy, and grace God had shown me in my past and present and had promised to show in my future.

I could not help but ask why. What did He see in me that prompted Him to take such interest in me and my future? Why does He continue to help me even though I do everything wrong? The Bible says, "God so loved the world, that he gave his only begotten Son, that who so ever believeth in him should not perish, but have everlasting life" (John 3:16). The answer is, it is because of His own love for me which is not dependent on anything that I do or don't do. As I thought on this matter, the words "thank you" were forced through my lips, and I began to cry all the more. In that moment, I realized that I was becoming who He saw me as even while I was walking in my corruption and unaware of who I was and when I kept turning my back on God. His love carried me to this point, and all at once it hit me. I was not only amazed but also humbled by his faithfulness to me. After that realization, I could not wait to write my speech.

I went home and began to reflect on what I wanted and needed to say. Since it wasn't my first speech, I had an idea of how to write it, but I knew I would have to give some thought to what to write. I awoke at six in the morning and after getting dressed I went straight to the coffee shop. Once I had my coffee, I began to type. To my surprise, the words just flowed through my mind the way water flows down a waterfall. I had a steady stream of ideas from the start until I was at the point where I felt satisfied with what I had written. I had intended for that copy to only be a rough draft; I wanted to keep going over it to make it better over the days to come. But as I allowed others to read it, they liked it so much that most of them thought it was the finished product—so besides a few minor changes, I decided to use it for the graduation speech.

Neither the significance of the speech nor the fact that I had earned a BA in psychology hit me until I attended the graduation rehearsal. At the rehearsal, I came face to face with the entire graduating class, and I was shocked. There were more than a hundred students, and out of all these people I was chosen to speak — Wow! I realized I had to be the very best I could be when I was called to the front to represent my class.

The day of graduation came faster than I wanted it to. When the day of May 13, 2017, came, I awoke with this sort of anticipation that filled my whole body with excitement. I jumped in and out of the bath and pulled out my tailor-made suit, feeling like I was going to be the belle of the ball. I thought, "Today, everyone I invited really knows my struggle because each one of them was instrumental at some point in my corruption"—there was Kim or K-Killer from Oakdale, who gave me the name of Freddy-Gz; there was my little brother David who ran the streets with me in the Nine Deep; there was Demetri and his brother Conrad, who were also members of the Nine Deep; and there was Auntie Sharon, and my best friend Tunisia, who has been with me through everything I had struggled through and overcome in my life. However, the most important people there were my two sons, Vonne and Jay, who also showed up to celebrate with me. As this was all an example to my children, my new life was dedicated to them—to prove to them that anything is possible if they are willing to work hard to earn it. Except for my daughters Anita and Adriana, who was one of my friends from San Francisco, everyone that I wanted to be there was there, and because of that I felt no anxiety about the speech.

As I approached my place, I recognized my friend Tai, a young lady on crutches, and as she saw me I gave her a smile. She smiled back and asked, "Frederick, you ready to represent?"

"You know it!"

We laughed together, and I said, "I want to thank you for voting for me. There is a part in my speech that I put in there just for you."

"What part? Come on, Frederick, what is it? Tell me so I'll know when I hear it."

"When you hear it, you'll know it," I assured her.

She said, "Alright, but it bet not be embarrassing."

"It won't, but I looked for your email so that you could have read it before today and given me some feedback."

"I'll give it to you before we leave today, okay."

"Alright, that's good. I'll look for you before I tear up out of here."

As Tai and I sat in the front row talking, the music began to play, and all the attention was turned to the stairs to the left of our seats. The procession of students began to walk down the stairs as the crowd stood to their feet. The noise was deafening—people were blowing horns, yelling, and clapping their hands together while music played over the loudspeaker. I felt so proud of the kids who were graduating, especially since there were a lot of African American young men and women who had earned their degrees. As the students were seated, I saw many of these young people standing and waving their hands at their families. Although I was happy for them, I silently wished that I had taken school seriously when I was young. I quickly dismissed those thoughts and just thanked God that I did it. Once everyone was seated in their places, the music stopped, and the master of ceremony took the stage.

The school had set up the graduation in front of the library at the center of the school. This was a very good spot for our graduation because of the way it was built. To the right and left of the school's library were stairs that would lead a person up to the very top of the school. These stairs were used for the graduates to make their walk to their seats as the music played. There was a big open space in front of the library that served as the seating for the graduating classes and the spectators. Above that area, there was another open space for family members to sit and people to stand as they watched the ceremony. The faculty were seated to the right of the stage, all of them wearing gowns and hoods that represented their program. On the stage were the regents of the school, the trustees, the school president, and the guest speaker. I did not pay much attention to the master of ceremony because I kept looking around and going over my speech in my head.

It wasn't that I was nervous—I just wanted to do a good job for my class because I believed this would be one of the last things they would remember of their days at the school. I wanted them to go out with inspiration and joy within their hearts and minds. After the master of ceremonies introduced the guest speaker, she stated that the student body president would be up next to introduce the student speakers. The guest speaker for the ceremony was the head of the Oakland branch of Kaiser Hospitals. To my surprise, he was a black man who had worked thirty-plus years within the medical world and had been in his present position for ten years. As he took the stage, I kind of drifted off and thought to myself, "Why don't people ever hear about black men and women who are doing great things like he has done?" I began to focus again as I saw the student president walking to the stage. Once again I began to repeat my speech to myself.

I was interrupted by the elation of the crowds as the student body president took the stage. He was a tall, white young man named James who had reddish hair, and as he faced the audience he wore a big smile. His first order of business was to greet us and the spectators, which he did with his hands raised high in the air. As he waved his hands, he shouted, "We did it!"

In response to his words, the graduates started to scream and wave their hands as well. Although I had not wanted to participate in the ceremony, as I sat there, I was glad that I had a change of heart. And as James began to introduce me, I bowed my head and said another silent thank-you to God.

Rolling up to the desk that I was to speak from, I instantly got energized. Turning to face the graduates, I stopped and looked over the entire crowd. Then I opened the folder that contained my speech and began to address the crowd. The pride that swept through my body as I spoke was consuming. Even as I was talking, I was thinking of my accomplishments and the significance of the moment. As a gang member, I was a leader and I was the one who spoke for the members. Now as an intellectual, I remained a leader. This realization forced me to accept the fact that the very thing that I thought furthered my corruption was one of the things that made me "me". Again, a value emerged: *never deny your past or turn from the attributes gained through corruption. Instead, embrace it as part of the journey that formed you and use everything that was learned to transform your character and help others.*

As I neared the end of my speech, I had to tell myself to slow down because I wanted to make a valuable point. I took a deep breath and said, "I challenge each of you to keep overcoming the odds and to shoot for the moon—because even if you miss the mark, you still will be among the stars."

The crowd erupted and most of the spectators were standing, but I just bowed my head and slowly rolled back to my place. Once I was done with my speech, the awarding of the diploma holders began.

I can't remember much of anything after I returned to my seat because I just sat staring at the many trees that surrounded the school, which were towering over the building behind the library. I thought to myself, *"Just as a redwood tree that plants its first roots into the ground has the possibility to grow one hundred or two hundred feet into the sky and stand for centuries, so have*

I planted my first roots into life. And as the redwood, I also have the possibility to reach heights that I have not imagined and stand for principles that I never knew existed." This thought brought a smile to my face and an overwhelming excitement to see what new goal would be accomplished in my future.

Chapter 12

The Lessons of My Past

Every principle I learned as a child, internalized as a youth, and manifested as a young adult could be seen in the thinking, actions, and motivations that placed me on that block, that night, and at that time. This statement is by no means meant to justify my actions or to diminish my choices, but it is to show how my choices were guided. When I began to value money in an environment where anything goes, it was only the lack of opportunity that kept me from taking it. Once I became strong, I was able to recognize those who were weak. With morals that said *to prey on the weak, take when you have the opportunity, and* blame the victim for their own *misfortune is the victim's fault,* everything I did seemed right at the time. That night in August I could have gone home, but with rent due, a baby to feed, and a woman to take care of, it was either that or suffer need—which at the time would have clashed with my moral at the time: *provide for your family no matter what the cost, and never be afraid to break the law to do so.*

At no time did I ever consciously make a decision based on what I had been taught. In each situation during my internalization and manifestation of corruption, I subconsciously reacted based not on what was "socially right" but on what I was taught was right, which was corrupt. No mother gives birth to a thug, criminal, or drug addict, but these types of people and their characters are formed by their experiences and environments. The stimuli that nourish a child are like seeds planted in the garden of his character. Whether his training is culturally, socially, or morally right or wrong, the child will receive it. In some cases, as in mine, the child does not have a right or wrong choice set before him, but is force-fed the wrong. The choices that he or she is given are more likely either bad or worse.

I could have chosen to not sell drugs, but for me, watching my little sister be tormented by her peers would have been far worse. When children have internalized corrupt morals and values, the lens in which they see the world is clouded; and unlike children who are raised with morals and values that are socially acceptable, they judge a situation by what's right for them rather than what's "socially right." Although my parents knew what was "socially right," they also knew they needed to provide, and it was that need that brought about all kinds of corruption.

The conditions and processes that produced and nourished the corruption within me are not unique to my family. Everyday within the ghettos of America, a child is going through a similar gauntlet, and his love and understanding are slowly being stamped out. In its place hatred, frustration, and anger are being nourished. Every moral and value that will be instilled within him will come by way of pain, disappointment, and poverty. Through these mediums his corruption is sure to form, and when he is of age, violence will be produced. By the time he is old enough to be incarcerated, all will label him a criminal—none will demonize the system that created the condition that formed him and kept him trapped within the ghetto with no resources.

Due to the oppression, racism, and blatant lack of concern by government officials for those within underrepresented neighborhoods, children are forgotten. They are left to fend for themselves, and all that is offered is crime. Some may say "why don't they just get a job," but at ten or twelve-years-of age, who will employ them? Even at that young age, because of their upbringing, they would feel inadequate, angry, and hurt, so they would look for comfort. But in the ghetto, the only role models are those who commit crimes and produce violence. It wasn't until I entered the church at the age of thirty-five that I even saw a man.

When I say "man," I mean those who are confident, intelligent, and proud of doing what is right. Those who have realized that it is not he who can physically dominate who is strong but he who is willing to be dominated for his righteous principles. Those who have correct values, morals, and principles governing their actions and words. This does not necessarily mean that they have conformed to the ruling class's ideals of what's right, but they have submitted to what God says is right. Through this understanding, they've come to value their compassion, love, and empathy for others. They realize these emotions are the ones that keep them connected to their brothers and sisters; they understand that it is through this connection that they can help, encourage, and change the generational trauma.

For the situations and traumatic experiences to be minimized in a child's life, we the African American race must seek to value each other. The lack of loving people in my life was one of the reasons that prompted me to hate others because as a child, I saw no one who actually cared about me. Resentment, anger, and frustrations overcame me and once filled, I gave it all back to the world through violence.

In many of the inner cities of this nation, children are still feeling the brunt of racism. Because of this, they are maturing in anger. To counteract their feelings of hopelessness, we must take the time to demonstrate to the child who has no outlet for his anger that there are those who care. If in my youth I had a responsible man or woman who could have taken the time to help me find my way through the frustrations of life and truly love me, who knows if it would have led me down another path.

There must be a paradigm shift where we draw the children of the ghetto away from a life of hopelessness, hate, and crime to one with confidence, love, and the accomplishment of their dreams. Most crimes are committed for money, so there must be opportunities within their reach. If there is no one at home to encourage them, then it must become our responsibility to do so. Those who were nourished within the ghetto but have risen above the tribulation and become educated and successful must return and set the example—so that generations who come after them have something to aspire to be. We must give to causes that aid those who are without means and support all schools no matter whether it's in your district or not. The simple fact is that it is education that will open the doors of the world to a child.

Yes, I do believe parents must play a role, but if they are incapable of leading the child in the right way, then those who are capable should take a prominent role in the child's training. These men and women could be teachers, preachers, elders of the church, coaches, neighbors, uncles, aunties, brothers, or sisters. They must challenge the child's mind and aid them in reaching their goals. A people divided against itself cannot stand, so we must come together and grow together as a people, as a nation, and as one race (the human race). Who knows? It may be that young African American child born in the ghetto, if loved and educated, who might just be the only one who can save your life one day.

THEMES

The Roar of an Uncaged Lion

1.) Choices one is forced to make because of poverty

2.) Internal battle between good and evil

3.) Learning to accept the consequences of bad decisions

4.) Understanding and dealing with mental illness

5.) Family being the first teacher

6.) Finding love and the pain of its loss

7.) True friendship and the grief that comes with the death of a friend

8.) The power of education

9.) The freedom that is found in religion

10.) Understanding one's self and one's own emotions

11.) One's ever changing perspectives concerning life

Discussion questions

What does Frederick suggest about the relationships between parents and children?

How did Frederick's home life prepare him to live the street life?

Does Frederick's injury change him? If so, how? If not, why not?

What were the reasons that led Frederick into the streets?

Was Frederick correct in thinking his only option to make money was to sell drugs? Could anything have prevented him from doing so?

How does jail change Frederick? How does he benefit from jail, and in what ways does it hurt him?

In Frederick's later years, what was the **triggering event** that led him to attend college?

Did Frederick's understanding of love change over time?

Essay Questions:

How did Frederick's male friendships change over time, and in what ways did they influence his life? (.ie age, influences, or helpfulness)

Did Frederick's perspectives on family, love, and character change over time? If so, how? If not, why not? What does this teach us about our own perspectives?

Describe the ways in which Frederick's growing spirituality created mental and emotional change in his life?

How was Frederick's relationship with his parents and siblings or his upbringing influential in how he raised his children and his relationships with women and his peers?

How do Frederick's struggles teach us about life, adversity, and resilience?

How were the women Frederick encountered throughout his life influential in his growth, understanding of himself, and achievements? Identify at least three women who were influential.

How did Frederick's lack of good role models and his having or not having a support system hurt or help him over the course of his life?

93675004R00163

Made in the USA
San Bernardino, CA
09 November 2018